Preaching and the Personal

Preaching and the Personal

Edited by
J. DWAYNE HOWELL

☙PICKWICK *Publications* · Eugene, Oregon

PREACHING AND THE PERSONAL

Copyright © 2013 Wipf and Stock Publishers. All rights reserved. Except for brief quotations in critical publications or reviews, no part of this book may be reproduced in any manner without prior written permission from the publisher. Write: Permissions. Wipf and Stock Publishers, 199 W. 8th Ave., Suite 3, Eugene, OR 97401.

Pickwick Publications
An Imprint of Wipf and Stock Publishers
199 W. 8th Ave., Suite 3
Eugene, OR 97401

www.wipfandstock.com

ISBN 13: 978-1-61097-826-2

Cataloguing-in-Publication data:

Preaching and the personal / edited by J. Dwayne Howell.

xii + 160 p. ; 23 cm. Includes bibliographical references.

ISBN 13: 978-1-61097-826-2

1. Preaching. 2. Hermeneutics—Religious aspects—Christianity. 3. Bible—Hermeneutics. 4. Bible—Homiletical use. I. Howell, J. Dwayne. II. Title.

BS534.5 P55 2013

Manufactured in the U.S.A.

Dedicated to the
Rolling Fork Baptist Church, Gleanings, Kentucky

Contents

Preface • ix
List of Contributors • xi
List of Abbreviations • xii

1 The Personal Nature of Preaching • 1
　—J. DWAYNE HOWELL

2 Preaching and the Personal • 11
　—ANNA CARTER FLORENCE

3 The Personal and Its Other in the Performance of Preaching • 19
　—RUTHANNA B. HOOKE

4 The Risk of Testimony • 44
　—WALTER BRUEGGEMANN

5 Collaborative Preaching and the Bible: Toward a Practical Theology of Memory • 56
　— JOHN S. MCCLURE

6 "It Ain't Necessarily So": Resistance Preaching and Womanist Thought • 71
　—VALERIE BRIDGEMAN

7   Liberating Preaching: Hispanic Hermeneutics and Homiletics: Collaborative and Contextual Approaches to Preaching • 80
    —DAVID CORTÉS-FEUNTES

8   Preaching John: The Word Made Flesh as Theological and Interpretive Method • 89
    —KAROLINE M. LEWIS

9   Scholars and Soccer Moms: Reflections on Objectivity and Subjectivity in Moving from Text to Sermon • 104
    —CHARLES L. AARON

10 Hearing the Voices of Others: A Collaborative Reading of Leviticus 19 • 121
    —J. DWAYNE HOWELL

11 Epilogue • 142
    —J. DWAYNE HOWELL

Appendix
Hispanic Biblical Hermeneutics and Homiletics: A Brief Bibliography • 145
—DAVID CORTÉS-FEUNTES

Bibliography • 151

Preface

PREACHING AND THE PERSONAL is a collection of papers that have been presented at the Society of Biblical Literature in sessions sponsored by the Homiletics and Biblical Studies section. The Homiletics and Biblical Studies section encourages dialogue among scholars in both fields who share an interest in critical exegesis, its various methods, and the unique hermeneutical and theological problems inherent to the relationship between biblical interpretation and proclamation. To this end the steering committee seeks to provide such dialogue through invited panels and open calls for presentation.

The concept for this book began with the panel discussion "Preaching and the Personal: Prophecy, Witness and Testimony" at the 2010 meeting in Atlanta. Papers presented by Walter Brueggemann and Anna Carter Florence at that meeting are included in this book. Additional writers who presented in other sessions of the Homiletics and Biblical Studies section were invited to submit their papers as well. Each paper explores various ways the personal can be found in the biblical text, in the preacher, and in the congregation. I want to thank the members of the steering committee, Charles L. Aaron, Ruthanna B. Hooke, Karoline M. Lewis, Dawn Ottoni-Wilhelm, and David Schnasa Jacobsen for their diligent work each year in planning the various sessions for the Society of Biblical Literature. I also want to thank them for encouraging me and contributing to the writing of *Preaching and the Personal*. Gratitude is also extended to all who contributed their essays to

Preface

be a part of the book. Each one has been gracious in accepting the opportunity to write a chapter and it has been a joy to get to know each one better through the process.

The majority of the editing for the book was done during my sabbatical leave in the Spring 2012. I appreciate President Michael V. Carter and the Trustees of Campbellsville University allowing me the opportunity for writing. Appreciation is also extended to my colleagues in the School of Theology of Campbellsville University who graciously filled in for my duties during my absence. I am also thankful for the support of my wife Dr. Susan Howell and children Katelyn and Patrick.

Pickwick Publications has provided excellent guidance through the writing process. In particular I want to thank Christian Amondson for his willingness and patience as I worked through the editing of the book.

Finally, I have dedicated the book to the Rolling Fork Baptist Church of Gleanings, Kentucky. Twice they have afforded me the opportunity to serve as their pastor. First, as a young seminary student (1984–1991) they guided me through the development of my ministry. Secondly, they allowed me to return in 2001 and I still serve as their pastor. I consider them, along with the members of its sister church, Highview United Methodist Church, family because of this time with them. We have shared in both our joys and our sorrows and understand the importance of the personal in preaching.

J. Dwayne Howell
Spring 2012

Contributors

Charles L. Aaron
Pastor
Whaley United Methodist Church
Gainesville, TX

Valerie Bridgeman
Associate Professor of Hebrew Bible/
 Homiletics and Worship
Scholar of Theology and the Arts
Lancaster Theological Seminary

Walter Brueggemann
Professor Emeritus
Columbia Theological Seminary

David Cortés-Fuentes
Pastor
Iglesia Presbiteriana Hispana
 Emmanuel
Claremont, CA

Anna Carter Florence
Peter Marshall Associate Professor of
 Preaching
Columbia Theological Seminary

Ruthanna B. Hooke
Associate Professor of Homiletics
Virginia Theological Seminary

J. Dwayne Howell
Professor of Old Testament and
 Hebrew
Campbellsville University

Karoline M. Lewis
Assistant Professor of Preaching
Luther Seminary

John S. McClure
Charles G. Finney Professor of
 Preaching and Worship
Vanderbilt Divinity School

Abbreviations

BDB	Brown, Driver, Briggs, *Hebrew and Aramaic Lexicon of the Old Testament*
KB	*The Hebrew and Aramaic Lexicon of the Old Testament: The New Koehler-Baumgartner*
NIB	*New Interpreter's Bible Commentary*
TDOT	*Theological Dictionary of the Old Testament*
TLOT	*Theological Lexicon of the Old Testament*

1

The Personal Nature of Preaching

J. DWAYNE HOWELL

PREACHING IS A PERSONAL event. Obviously, it involves the individual preparation and presentation by a minister or speaker. However, preaching also includes the Bible as a central source. This source comes from and provides a basis for the believing community. The preaching event is also personal for the members of the congregation. They are not simply receptors of the preacher's words based on a biblical text. The congregation is also involved personally in how each individual interprets the words and the text. What is said in the text, what is said in the sermon, and the listener's response comprise parts of each one's testimony. Anna Carter Florence defines testimony as "both a narration of events and a confession of belief: we tell what we have seen and heard, and we confess what we believe about it."[1] Testimony runs throughout the Bible, preaching, and the congregation. It is in this interchange of text, preacher, and listener that not just one testimony develops but many testimonies are present.

1. Florence, *Preaching as Testimony*, xiii.

Preaching and the Personal

THE PERSONAL AND THE BIBLE

The Bible is the witness of faith communities that has been shared for generations, the testimonies of the ones who have come before us. The stories of the Bible convey the journey of faith that the believing communities experienced, and handed down through both oral and written traditions. James A. Sanders calls this the canonical process and includes not only the development of the written text but also the intertextuality of the text and the unrecorded hermeneutics that are part of the development of the canon.[2] The human element of the text should not be denied. Manfred T. Baruch believes that the nature of Scripture includes both divine inspiration and human reception.

> This means that the Bible, despite the limitation of the human writers—which include the possibility of misunderstanding, mishearing, or only partially hearing and understanding the revelatory speaking and acting of God—is trustworthy and perfectly sufficient for the redemptive, life-and-world-transfoming purpose for which God inspired it.[3]

In the process of developing the Biblical story the writers used various literary methods, wrote in a particular culture, and developed their testimonies. These testimonies were not intended to simply report past events, but instead they served as a means to provide hope for future generations. In his essay, "Story and History in Biblical Theology," James Barr emphasizes that the narrative in the Old Testament is closer to story than it is to history. Borrowing a term from Hans Frei, he calls biblical narratives "history-like."[4] He does not deny that the narratives have any relation to history. Instead, he sees story as moving in and out of history but not relying purely on history. He continues in his essay, "Historical Reading and Theological Interpretation," to provide the purpose of biblical narrative.

---

2. Sanders, *From Sacred Story to Sacred Text*, 61–62. See also Sanders, *Canon and Community*, 21–45.

3. Brauch, *Abusing Scripture*, 23.

4. Frei, *The Eclipse of Biblical Narrative*, 8–12.

He believes that the narratives were not written primarily out of an interest in the past; they were written for a quite different reason:
1) They can be written to provide pictures of the promises of God which will come to pass in the future.
2) Even if their literal purpose concerns the past, their theological function and purpose may be directed toward the future.[5]

Thus, Barr maintains that the biblical writers are not viewed as writing mere "records" of past events, but instead they are seen as writing "paradigms" for the present that point to the future.[6] Sanders refers to this as the "adaptability" of the text. While the text provides a tradition, it also has the ability to be adapted to the readers on sociological setting.

> The primary characteristic of canon, therefore, is its adaptability. Israel's canon was basically a story adaptable to a number of different literary forms, adaptable to the varying fortunes of the people who found their identity in it, adaptable to widely scattered communities themselves adjusting to new or strange idioms of existence but retaining a transitional identity, and adaptable to a sedentary or migratory life.[7]

The adaptability of the text also allows for disagreement over the meaning of the text. Being personal, a testimony of what one sees and hears in the text, can lead to differences in meaning with others. These differences can be found both in the text and in the interpretation of the text. Walter Brueggemann refers to this as "testimony" and "counter-testimony." He speaks of a "second listening community" in Old Testament theology:

> Thus the enterprise of Old Testament theology is put, I believe inescapably, in a situation where exposition is always conducted in the presence of two audiences.

---

5. Barr, *The Scope and Authority of the Bible*, 36.

6. Ibid. See also Barr, "Some Thoughts on Narrative, Myth, and Incarnation." Barr states, "The motivation of much Israelite storytelling was not to discuss or to relate how things had been long ago but to provide accounts of things as they now are or to provide paradigms for future hope."

7. Sanders, *From Sacred Story to Sacred Text*, 19.

Preaching and the Personal

> In the first instant, exposition is directed at the self-understanding, self-discernment, and authorization of the community that begins in assent to this text... (and) a second listening community: the larger public that is willing to host many alternative construals of reality.[8]

This "alternative construal of reality" is not limited to the text, but can also be found in the minister's interpretation of the text in the sermon and the hearer's interpretation of the sermon and text.

THE PERSONAL AND THE PREACHER

How one interprets the biblical text is also personal. Often I hear the frustration of my students when I teach hermeneutics—"I just want to study the Word!" However, when we come to study the Bible we do not come to it *de nova*—with nothing. To simply say "the text means what the text means" is often a one-dimensional understanding of the Bible. Sadly, often we want it to mean *what we* want it to mean. When hearing, reading, and interpreting the text, we bring our own selves to the text, both the preacher and the congregation. This includes:

1) *Our culture*, which includes how we were raised and where we were raised;
2) *Our beliefs*, based on our faith development and maturity;
3) *Our personality*, and our understanding of the role of personality and how we view the world;
4) *Our prejudices*, a pre-judgment of the text, already knowing what we want the Scripture to say.

Every time one studies the Bible, he or she is making decisions concerning the interpretation of the text based on these and other factors. Just as the biblical writers could misunderstand, mishear, or only partially hear and understand "the revelatory speaking and acting of God," so can the minister in interpreting the text. Craig Dykstra believes that in the life of the congregation we often engage

---

8. Brueggemann, *Theology of the Old Testament*, 87.

in "socially acceptable (indeed, socially celebrated) patterns of self destruction." This includes the minister and preaching. People can tend to manipulate others to serve their own purpose and achievement. In doing so, it destroys what a person needs most—unconditional love—and the church has to be a place of unconditional love. This requires giving up our own "self-security"(achievement [overcoming chaos] made on our own) for faith (trusting God for security [who has overcome chaos]).[9]

Students are taught methods of exegesis and hermeneutics in order to discern the meaning of a given text. Often such work emphasizes the historical nature of the text, what a text *meant*. However, hermeneutics should also emphasize what a text *means*, how the text is adaptable to the current situaiton. My students often find difficulty in determining what a text *means*. Several reasons can be given for this problem of application including a lack of knowledge of current events, fear of making an incorrect interpretation, going against what they have been taught either in church or in school, and misjudging the current situation.

A challenge that faces both the seasoned minister and the student is being able to apply the appropriate word for the appropriate situation. One characteristic both true and false prophets shared in common in the Old Testament was that they both said, "Thus saith the Lord," claiming divine sanction for their words. Again testimony and counter-testimony can be found in sermons throughout the ages. In a study of preaching in the pro-slavery south, James O. Farmer states: "Thus it was a simple matter for Southern churchmen to conceive of the slavery debate as a struggle between pious Christian orthodoxy and the modern ideology they came to call rationalism, with the soul of American society at stake."[10] Social issues, including gay rights, are currently being contested in churches. Church leaders from both sides debate the "proper biblical understanding" of the text, claiming others use an inappropriate hermeneutic.[11]

---

9 Dykstra, *Growing in the Life of Faith*, 14, 86–87.
10. Farmer, *The Metaphysical Confederacy*, 206.
11. Allen, "Baptists Split on NC Gay Marriage Ban."

Preaching and the Personal

THE PERSONAL AND THE CONGREGATION

The critically studied text needs to be applied to the context of the faith community. James A. Sanders states:

> The Bible, whatever canonical content, has its true *Sitz im Leben* in church or synagogue, not the scholar's study. The Bible has tremendous value, as archaeologists and other historians have shown, for reconstructing history; and it has other secular values. But it has another dimension that gives it a qualitative difference from being only a source book. Despite its considerable pluralism it came out of early believing communities over a two-thousand year period and it still belongs there.[12]

He believes the emphasis on the Enlightenment in biblical studies has locked the text in the past—"chained to the scholar's desk"[13]—and views the responsibility of the minister to be like the beadle "who carries the critically studied Bible procession back to the church lectern from the scholar's study."[14] A similar image is used by Thomas Long: the preacher as "witness."[15] Long states that the preacher "theologically" comes "from *within* the community of faith and not *to* it from the outside."[16]

I first became aware of the personal nature of preaching in reading *Tracks of a FellowStruggler* by John Claypool. The book is a collection of sermons preached by Claypool that deal with the diagnosis of acute leukemia and the eventual death of his ten-year old daughter Larua Lue. In the sermons Claypool bore his own personal and family struggles. Yet the sermons are not simply focused on him, but are a journey of faith that he invited his congregations to travel with him. This style of preaching is called confessional preaching. In *The Preaching Event*, Claypool states: "We will make our greatest impact in preaching when we dare to make available

---

12 *From Sacred Story to Sacred Text*, 193.
13. Ibid., 157.
14. Sanders, *Canon and Community*, 20.
15. Long, *The Witness of Preaching*.
16. Ibid., 10.

to the woundedness of others what we have learned through honest grappling with our own woundedness."[17] How the congregation receives the testimony of the sermon can also vary from acceptance to rejection. Part of the risk of testimony is that others may reject what is said.[18] Writing in the preface to *Tracks of a FellowStruggler*, Claypool shares:

> As one would expect, sermons of this nature evoked a variety of response. Some people were frankly offended at the notes of ambiguity and anger which I openly acknowledged. They obviously felt that preachers were to deal with "answers" and not "questions." One seminary professor even murmured that the third sermon bordered on heresy. At the same time, many other people acknowledged being helped by some, if not all, of these words.[19]

The beadle, the witness, and confessional preaching together provide an image of the preacher's role in the delivery of the sermon. However, what of the experience, the testimony of the congregation—better yet, what of the testimonies of the congregation? The congregation, like the minister comes to the sermon with its own baggage—culture, education, personality, and prejudice. The listeners have their own stories of faith and their own questions. Those who were a part of the "Listening to the Listener" project noted: "People who regularly hear sermons in a congregation do not hear sermons in a vacuum."[20]

How does the congregation relate to the text and the sermon? Just as the text and the minister have a context, so does each member of the congregation. The preacher is taught not only to exegete the text but also to exegete the congregation, to know the congregation. This includes knowing the way people learn,[21] their

---

17. Claypool, *The Preaching Event*, 86–87.

18. Long, *Testimony: Talking Ourselves into Being Christian*, 3. Long says that "speaking about faith in public always runs the risk of offense or even social rejection," ibid.

19. Claypool, *Tracks of a FellowStruggler*, 14–15.

20. McClure, et al., *Listening to the Listener: Homiletical Case Studies*, 6.

21. Troeger and Everding, *So That All Might Know*.

personalities,[22] and even their cultural contexts.[23] It would be difficult to try to address each situation in every sermon, still an understanding of the congregation aids in both the preparation and delivery of the sermon.

While there are ways for the minister to better know the congregation, how can the congregation share its own testimony? The call and response style has long been associated with African-American preaching.[24] In an interesting turn on the call and response, some churches are having members text questions during the sermon that the pastor answers at the end of the message.[25] Other churches host a "pastor chat," often after the service, where members can discuss the pastor's sermon. However, these still center on the pastor and his or her interpretation of the text and delivery of the sermon. One way, advocated by John S. McClure, allows people to become a part of the sermon preparation process, what he calls collaborative preaching.[26] This method seeks to involve the congregation and community in the sermon development and delivery process through work groups that meet regularly with the pastor. Another way to allow the congregation to participate in the personal is to teach the members how to each share his or her testimony, what has been seen and heard and believed.[27]

CONTINUING THE DISCUSSION

The following essays continue the discussion of *Preaching and the Personal*. In the next chapter, "Preaching and the Personal," Anna Carter Florence continues the concept of testimony that she writes about in her book, *Preaching as Testimony*. She reminds her students that "God may be the subject (of the sermon—mine), but

22. Baab, *Personality Type in Congregations*.

23. Segovia, *Decolonizing Biblical Studies*; Dietrich and Luz, *The Bible in a World Context*.

24. Crawford, *The Hum*.

25. Charles, "Thumb Wars."

26. McClure, *The Round-Table Pulpit*.

27. Daniel, *Telling It Like It Is*.

you, the preacher, will be laid bare in the sermon." She speaks about the concept of "the logic of *leiros*" found in Luke 24:11 and how it should affect the preacher.

Ruthanna B. Hooke addresses the personal element of preaching in, "The Personal and Its Other in the Performance of Preaching." Applying performance theory to preaching, she speaks to how the person of the preacher is strongly present in the preaching event.

Walter Brueggemann, in his essay, "The Risk of Testimony," uses readings from Second Isaiah to "break the silence," both in the biblical context and in the modern day situation.

John S. McClure speaks to the rise of reception-oriented homiletics, the process of receiving and using the sermon by the congregation, in his chapter, "Collaborative Preaching and the Bible: Toward a Practical Theology of Memory."

The next two essays deals with how the personal crosses cultural boundaries. First, Valerie Bridgeman Davis provides an introduction to Womanist theory in biblical interpretation in her essay, "'It Ain't Necessarily So': Resistance Preaching and Womanist Thought." David Cortés-Feuntes offers a primer on the rise of preaching from a Latino/a perspective in his essay, "Liberating Preaching: Hispanic Hermeneutics and Homiletics: Collaborative and Contextual Approaches to Preaching." (A bibliography of recent works in Hispanic Hermeneutics and Homiletics is provided in Appendix A.)

The final three chapters provide hermeneutical and homiletical examples of preaching and the personal. Each chapter offers a study of a biblical text, the use of a method of interpreatation, and closes with a sermon based on the research. In her essay, "Preaching the Word of John: The Word Made Flesh as Theological and Interpretive Method," Karoline M. Lewis speaks of the importance of "rereading" the text and focusing on the process of reading and not simply the result of reading. Charles L. Aaron applies the work of Anna Carter Florence to his study of John 12:1–11 in his essay, "Scholars and Soccer Moms: Reflections on Objectivity and Subjectivity in Moving from Text to Sermon." The final essay by J. Dwayne Howell, "Hearing the Voice of Others: A Collaborative Reading of

Preaching and the Personal

Leviticus 19," studies the treatment of the immigrant found in Leviticus 19:33 and 34, using a collaborative approach.

2

Preaching and the Personal

ANNA CARTER FLORENCE

FIRST OFF, LET ME say how delighted I was to learn that there is a homiletics workgroup at the Society for Biblical Literature. It isn't a self-evident reality. You probably know that. Studying the text is often preferable to talking about it in public.

I teach preaching, which is not something that is easy to tell people who are sitting next to you on airplanes. It is also not an easy thing to explain to one's colleagues, even in a theological education setting. I will never forget a conversation I once had with a man I like and respect, a religion scholar and a person of deep faith, who asked me, with genuine curiosity, "So—what is it you *do*, exactly, when you teach preaching? Do you teach them to talk?" I don't remember what I said in reply. Now I would probably say something like, "Yeah, that's probably accurate: I teach them to talk. About God. Every week. Whether they want to or not."

This is the first point I want to make. *Preachers talk about God, not themselves, because God is the subject, not the preacher.* That is rule number one, the preacher's greatest commandment. And while it sounds simple enough to make a student roll her eyes, it is not; oh, no. I tell my students that remembering this will be the great existential battle of their lives, because the temptation to change the subject from GOD to YOU is constant and fierce. Here is its most typical expression. The preacher is reading the text, studying the text, pleading with the text (to give her a sermon, that is), and suddenly, she sees something that leaps up from the page. In my context, we call this a movement of the spirit, because we're pretty sure that whatever leaped up and caught the preacher's attention is a gift, pure and simple; it isn't that the preacher suddenly got smarter and therefore was rewarded with insight. No, it feels more arbitrary than that, as anyone who has wrestled with a text knows. So the preacher has this *moment* of insight and gift, when she suddenly *knows* that a few minutes ago, she had nothing, and now, she is going to have a sermon; she has *conceived*, and almost immediately, the battle begins. *Wait a minute,* she thinks. *I can't say that. If I say that, what will they think? What will they say? What will they do to me?*—and before you can say "SBL," she has changed the subject, from God, to herself. It renders her mute, and her sermon lifeless. I think it is the reason so many of our faith communities are shrinking. Who wants to come watch a preacher violate rule number one, week after week? And they will see it. The congregation will see the preacher changing the subject from God to herself, so that she is protected from all that can happen to a person who dares to speak about God.

Which leads me to the second point I want to make. Ironically, subversively, rule number one is intimately connected to rule number two, which states that *God may be the subject, but you, the preacher, will be laid bare in the sermon.* The sermon is personal. Interpretation is personal. You cannot engage a text and emerge without a limp or a scar or some other trace of what that text did to you. And when you preach after such an encounter, *that* is what the congregation will see. They will see that you were brave and crazy enough to hang in there with whatever leaped up at you in the first place, instead of retreating in fear and shame and the hope of self-preservation. They will see that you cared more about pointing to God than saving yourself and your reputation.

So preaching is personal. Oh, yes. The sermon is practically a blueprint of the preacher. It may not show you the narrative minutiae of the preacher's day—what he bought at the grocery store, the fight he had with his kid before lunch, etc., etc.—and the preacher may never actually say a word about himself, but his sermon will show us the important things. It will show us what he is willing to look at, and what he is not. It will show us how deeply he is willing to go with something, and where he slams on the brakes and backs right up. The sermon is an x-ray scanner, and maybe even a TSA pat-down, of the preacher as interpreter, and *that* gets personal, very fast.

So how is a preacher to navigate rule number one and rule number two, without sliding into the sermon as a vehicle for entertainment or lecture or blog or twitter or perhaps the worst of all: "Happy Prayer-of-Jabez Preaching"? Here is what I offer my students: I offer them the tradition of testimony.

Now, testimony is a word that is laden with meanings, so let me clarify some terms. By "testimony" I do not mean "telling your story" or "using personal illustrations," nor am I suggesting that the sermon is an appropriate vehicle for the preacher's memoirs. Instead, I am drawing on the classical definition of testimony as both a narration of events and a confession of belief: we tell what we have seen and heard, and we confess what we believe about it. A sermon in the testimony tradition is not an autobiography, but a very particular kind of proclamation: the preacher tells what she has seen and heard *in the biblical text and in life*, and then confesses what she believes about it. Furthermore—and this is the troublesome part for preachers—there is no proof for testimony other than the engagement of a witness, and no proof for a sermon other than the engagement of the preacher. It is impossible to prove whether a sermon is true or false. One can only believe it or reject it.

Let me say a quick word about sources for my own work in testimony. The two major ones are Walter Brueggemann and Paul Ricoeur. Ricoeur's classic essay, "The Hermeneutics of Testimony," argues that Christian interpreters must choose testimony as their distinctive hermeneutic or they risk sliding into a hermeneutic of

Preaching and the Personal

absolute certainty, which, for a witness, is impossible.[1] Brueggemann's *Theology of the Old Testament*, which appeared the year I was beginning my dissertation on testimony (and which I think is the most important work for homiletics in thirty years), argues that testimony is the distinctive mode of speech in the Hebrew Bible (and, by extension, the New Testament): Israel speaks of God in both core testimony (God is great and God is good), and countertestimony (God may be great, and God may be God, but God sure isn't acting in character now, so get with the program), which must be held together, lest God become an idol.[2] I have also drawn on feminist scholarship, in particular Rebecca Chopp and Mary McClintock Fulkerson.[3] From them, I have developed a proposal for another view of the role of experience in proclamation: the preacher is called to engage the liberating power of God's Word in the biblical text and in life, and then to narrate and confess what she has seen and believed in that experience.

But perhaps the most telling sources for my work in testimony have been the human subjects: preachers themselves. I have spent a lot of time studying historical women preachers—who, I am happy to tell you, *do* exist, and in great numbers, because why on earth would we ever think that people only preach when they have *permission* to do so! So I have studied them, for what they can teach us about testimony, and their willingness to stand up and say what they see and believe in scripture and in life, no matter the consequences. I have also spent a lot of time in Christian churches, talking to pastors and congregations about their desire to speak of God and freedom and liberation and oppression. They have things to say, but they don't always know how to start. Because, before they can talk about God, they have to remember the times they *didn't* talk about God, the times they kept silent, and so participated in changing the subject.

What I have learned in my work with human subjects in the church is that people are clamoring to talk about God in more

1. Ricoeur, "The Hermeneutics of Testimony."
2. Brueggemann, *Theology of the Old Testament*.
3. Chopp, *The Power to Speak*; McClintock Fulkerson, *Changing the Subject*.

modes (testimony and counter-testimony, for example) than they knew were available, and over a broader sweep of time. They would *like* to talk about where they have seen God this past week, to offer the community a testimony, but they aren't always ready to do it. Because, what they are mulling over is how their encounter with God *this* week totally disrupts the encounter they thought they had last year, or ten years ago, or fifty years ago. People want to talk about how their God-talk has changed—how *they* have changed. And that takes some courage.

Peter knew about this. In Luke's gospel, the women run from the tomb on Easter morning with an unbelievable message about a stone rolled away, two men in dazzling clothes, and *resurrection*, of all things. The disciples are less than thrilled and less than receptive: "But these words seemed to them an idle tale, and they did not believe them" (Luke 24:11). The verse makes it sound as if the disciples simply dismissed the women's words as chattering foolishness. But the Greek word *leros* (wistfully translated here as "idle tale") actually means "garbage," "trash," "drivel," nonsense," or, to push the metaphor, @#$%!&@*. It is the only time the word appears in the New Testament; it is meant to shock, to make a singular gash across the text. Luke is driving home the point that Peter and the rest of the disciples don't just *ignore* the women; they *insult* them and mock them with words that are meant to hurt: *Resurrection! You're so full of @#$%!&!* Yet in the very next verse, we read that Peter got up and ran to the tomb, and stooping and looking in, he saw the linen cloths by themselves, and went home, amazed at what had happened (v. 12).

This, I think, is the logic of *leros*: when we speak of resurrection, we are not supposed to be believed. When we tell where we have seen God, those who love us and love God most will reject us outright—because they have to go look for themselves.

Peter had to go look for himself. It's a pattern that carries a certain familiarity, given his history: first Peter denies Jesus, and then he denies his friends. He is concerned about his own protection, his own reputation, his own worldview (*resurrection is impossible!*), his own survival. Who can blame him? If the women's words are true, then Peter has a task ahead of him: resurrection comes with consequences. He will need to engage in the work of truth and reconciliation before his broken relationships with his Lord and his friends can be healed. He will need to change the subject from himself to God, and thus reveal more about himself than he can bear. How tempting to yell "*Leros!*" with the crowd and deny what is inevitably ahead of him! And so he succumbs, as we all succumb. The resurrecting power of God will always overturn our little worlds, and the logic of *leros* is our human instinct to kill the messenger who brings word of it.

Some time ago I visited a church in Prince Edward County, Virginia. Prince Edward County came to national attention in 1951 over segregation laws, when students at one of the black high schools staged a walk-out to protest the miserable conditions at their school. Their case became one of five incorporated in *Brown vs. Board of Education,* which eventually resulted in the desegregation of public schools in 1954. Prince Edward County, however, was fierce in its refusal to comply with the new desegregation laws. In order to prevent black and white students from sitting in the same classrooms, the county shut down its entire school system for five years, the only school district in the nation to do so. So from 1959 to 1964, African American children in Prince Edward County had no access to any public education. They had to leave home to live with friends or relatives in other states just to go to school.

Only a handful of white residents spoke out against what was happening in Prince Edward County at the time. One of them was the local minister of the church I happened to be visiting, and for this, he lost his job. The church fired him, and opened its building for white students to use as classrooms while the town built a segregation academy for whites only.

This is a horrific history, and the people of Prince Edward County are only beginning to learn that they need to talk about it. The church I visited, however, is less sure. How do you talk about terrible things that happened more than sixty years ago? How do you explain the fact that the local segregation academy began in a church—*your* church? No matter how much time has passed, no matter how different you are, it's still hard to talk about. And so the people of this little church haven't really begun the work of truth and reconciliation. They live, for the most part, by a rule my Virginia grandmother often counseled: *if you can't say something nice, don't say anything at all*. But that makes for a lot of silence, and silence kills the human spirit.

The pastor of this little church in Prince Edward County asked me to speak about testimony, and so we talked about *Ieros* and Peter and how even those who resist the Word most may come to preach it one day themselves. And suddenly it hit me: these people need Peter. They need the space he opens up for them as a model for massive sin and massive repentance. They need to see disciples who utterly failed, and then found their way back. The logic of *Ieros*.

So I told them a piece of my own history. My great grandfather was a minister in the Cumberland Presbyterian Church and a singing evangelist. He was also, I recently learned, a member of the Ku Klux Klan when he was a young man. That was in the years when the KKK resurfaced, and actively recruited members, until in some areas of the Midwest, as many as one in five young white men were members. And for a brief period, my great grandfather was one of those.

The family never talked about it. It's not nice stuff to talk about, you know: Racist, anti-Semitic, anti-Catholic, anti-immigrant, anti-communist, USA-all-the-way extremism. Unspeakably awful.

But here's the weird part. My great grandfather went on to raise a son who became a civil rights preacher. His son and namesake, my great uncle, was a Presbyterian pastor who was active in the civil rights movement in Ohio in the 1950s and 1960s, and whose last act as a pastor, before he retired, was to test ordination laws in the church by ordaining an openly gay man as an elder.

I have asked myself: how could this happen? How could my family change the way it talked about God over the years, so that we went from the KKK to civil rights?

I don't know the answer to that, but I suspect it has to do with *Ieros*. I suspect that somewhere, at some moment, my great-grandfather realized that he had utterly rejected a testimony of resurrection. He had said "*Ieros*" to a vision of freedom for all people, and he had denied his own Lord. Like Peter. And that is a hell of a place to live, literally. It's a locked room, and you can hide out there for years. Until you decide to go to the tomb and see for yourself.

At some point, my great grandfather's testimony changed. What he saw and believed about God changed. His son heard it, and spent *his* life testifying to freedom.

I have come to wonder if the greatest gift testimony offers to the faith community is a way to speak about God over time. We are going to be lousy witnesses, sometimes. We are going to totally screw up. We will change the subject from God to ourselves and we will talk about our own power instead of the liberation and resurrection. We will say unspeakable things, and practice all those verbs that Peter excelled at: *deny, desert, reject, refuse.*

This is the logic of *leros*. Time passes—three days might even be enough—and resurrection happens. You see and believe and talk about God differently, because testimony opens up space to see God in the very places where we have viciously and vociferously denied that God can be. It is not a pardon. It is not a get-out-of-jail-free card. It is a way to begin the slow, hard work of truth and reconciliation which is the work of being human. And, incidentally, it is the work of becoming a preacher, because you can't preach unless you've said *leros* first.

Preaching is personal, oh yes. If my students knew *how* personal, they might never dare to try. But we have to. Testimony, as Brueggemann says, is our mother tongue.[4] It may also be our best hope for breaking the silences of this world.

---

4. Brueggemann, *Theology of the Old Testament*, 746–47.

3

The Personal and Its Others in the Performance of Preaching

RUTHANNA B. HOOKE

A FORMER STUDENT ONCE told me a story about how she deals with her fears when she is about to preach. She said that when she was a child and was nervous about serving for the first time as an acolyte in a worship service, the priest with whom she was serving comforted her by saying, "Remember, they didn't come here to see you." She told me that she remembers these words and is still calmed by them when she is about to step into the pulpit.

This comment—"they didn't come here to see you"—brings to the fore the complex question of the role of the personal in preaching. This has been a vexed question for homileticians, provoking a wide range of positions about such matters as the role of personal stories in the sermon.[1] The question about the role of the personal in preaching is a question about the status of the "you" in this comment. Is this "you" the focus of the sermon or not? In what way is

---

1. See, among many examples, Lischer, *A Theology of Preaching*; and Florence, *Preaching as Testimony*, for two differing positions on the role of the personal in preaching.

this "you" to be present or not to be present? What is the role of this "you" in the preaching event? This statement—"they didn't come here to see you"—points to three interrelated factors influencing these questions. First, the comment implies that the hearers have come to see someone else other than the preacher—namely, God. The comment thus points to the hope that many listeners have when they hear a sermon, which is that they will not only be encountering a human speaker but will encounter God in this event. Second, the very fact that this comment is made indicates that there is in fact a strongly personal presence in the sermon—the "you" that the hearers are supposedly not here to see is actually very much a factor in the sermon. Third, the comment suggests that this presence of the personal is problematic, such that it needs to be dismissed with some force. If the personal were not often felt to be an impediment to the sermon, it would not be necessary to state that it is *not* the focus of the sermon. These three implications of the comment suggest that the presence of the personal in preaching needs to be more fully thought through than this comment allows. To locate the place of the personal is more complicated than either saying it does not matter to the sermon, or else saying it is to be present in an un-nuanced way.

In this paper I will argue that the personal element of preaching, the preacher herself, is a necessary aspect of the preaching event and should not be minimized. Even if the hearers have ultimately come to see and hear God, this revelation takes place, paradoxically, precisely through the personal—through the particularity of the preacher as it is manifest in the sermon. This essay will argue that, indeed, the listeners *have* come to see "you," the preacher, and thereby to see God through "you." It is true, however, that the role of the personal is complex and prone to abuse, and thus it is important that preachers understand their personal role in a way that enhances, rather than detracts from, the preaching event. This way of being personally present in preaching is somewhat counterintuitive, hence it is often easier simply to dismiss the personal out of hand. Rather than doing this, I will employ a framework for understanding the self-other relationship taken from performance theory. This framework, I propose, suggests ways that the dialectical relationship between preacher and God, preacher and text, and preacher and hearers can be inhabited such that the personal in relation to these "others" becomes the vehicle for revelation rather than an impediment to it.

WHAT, THEN, HAVE WE COME OUT TO SEE?

The comment, "they didn't come here to see you," raises the question of what, precisely, those who attend sermons have come to see and hear. What are our hopes for the event of preaching? One way to describe our hope for proclamation is that, as the preacher negotiates the relationship between text and context, the sermon that results will not only be human speech about God but that, in the midst of this human speech, God will also speak. This theological claim can be put in a variety of ways: God reveals Godself in preaching; God makes Godself present in preaching; preaching is God's Word. To say that preaching is inspired is also to make a version of this claim, since the root of this word means "to be breathed into." What is it that breathes into us but the Holy Spirit, the *ruach*, the divine breath? To be an inspired preacher is to be breathed into by the Holy Spirit, and hence to say that preaching is inspired is another way of pointing to God's presence in the sermon. Most Christian theologies of preaching argue that, although all aspects of life can mediate God's presence and be revelatory of God, preaching does this in a privileged way. Preaching is paired with the sacraments as a pre-eminent event through which God reveals Godself. Although historically it has been Protestant theologians who have made this claim most strongly, in recent years Roman Catholic thinkers have also reclaimed a robust theology of the Word, and made a more central place for preaching as a revelatory event alongside the sacraments.[2] The claim that God speaks in preaching is usually linked to the preaching of scripture: preaching is the Word of God to the extent that it bears witness to the Bible's witness.

---

2. See, for instance, Rahner, "Priest and Poet"; and Rahner, "The Word of God and the Eucharist."

Preaching and the Personal

To claim that preaching is or can be an event in which God speaks raises the question of the preacher's role in the preaching event, the place of the personal in preaching. If the human preacher and her words are the media through which God speaks and reveals Godself, what does she need to do and to be in this event? What are the implications for the preacher's words, her bearing, her attitude toward her hearers, if she is caught up in this revelatory event? This question is important precisely because the person of the preacher is strongly present in the preaching event. The sermon is arguably the most personal part of the worship service, more personal (which is not to say more intimate) than the readings from scripture or the Eucharist. The sermon is the most personal part of the service in that it is here that the liturgical event is most inflected by a personality (that of the preacher), most mediated through a specific human being. Here we use our own words, rather than the words of others, to explore and mediate the Christian tradition and mystery. The sermon is also personal in that it is the part of the service probably most inflected by the specific congregation in which it takes place, which is another way of saying that sermons are always highly contextual, created for a certain community at a certain point in time, while the scriptures and other elements of the liturgy tend to be more universal.

Karl Barth famously argues that, because the sermon is an event in which God speaks, the personal element in preaching should be minimized as much as possible. Barth's primary metaphor for the preacher is that of a "herald" who proclaims a word he has received from the king, a word that is not the herald's own and that is not shaped or inflected by his own history, experience, social location, or perspective. Barth describes the human task in preaching in this way:

> If the human word of preaching is to perform the service of leading to the hearing of God's Word . . . It must be a selfless human word, a human word which will not say this or that in a spirit of self-assertion, but devote itself only to letting God's own Word say what must be said. Like a window, it must be a transparent word; or like a mirror, a reflecting word. The more it . . . rejects anything

> which might intervene as a third element between God's Word and the human hearer, the less it obtrudes itself in its own solidity between God and the hearer, the more it is positively an indication . . . and compulsion to hearing the Word of God itself, and negatively a hushing of all possible notes of false idolatry and human exaltation—the better it will be.[3]

Barth limits the role of the personal in preaching in a radical way, insisting that the preacher's "solidity" does not belong in the sermon—meaning not just their opinions and perspective but also, in a sense, all aspects of their human particularity. Instead, the preacher should be a transparent pane of glass, or a mirror reflecting the divine, intruding herself as little as possible into the preaching event.

In this directive of Barth's, the personal is to be minimized in preaching not simply in order to allow God's voice to be heard but still more because there is a sense that the personal, the human element, is positively an obstacle to God's being heard if this element is not strictly curbed. Barth appears sensitive to the fact that the sermon is a strongly personal event, and worries that this powerful, personal element in preaching too easily becomes "self-assertion," an expression of "false idolatry and human exaltation" that can only "obtrude" into the meeting between God and the hearer. Clearly for Barth the personal is problematic in preaching.

Barth's construal of the place of the personal in preaching has been much critiqued, on the ground that he does not take either the hermeneutical process or the incarnation seriously enough.[4] Regarding the incarnation, Barth argues that God's self-revelation occurred paradigmatically in the life, death, and resurrection of Jesus Christ, and that this revelation ought to be the model for all events of revelation that follow, including preaching. However, if the incarnation is the model for all of God's acts of self-revelation, this suggests that God reveals Godself not by bypassing humanity but by inhabiting humanity, in this case the particular, historical,

---

3. Barth, *Church Dogmatics* 1/2, 764.

4. See, for instance, Long, *The Witness of Preaching*, 19–28; and Wilson, *The Practice of Preaching*, 95.

and embodied human existence of Jesus of Nazareth. God's revelation occurs in and through what is human, not by the effacement of the human. Applied to preaching, this would mean that the Word of God is spoken in preaching when that Word meets the historical, particular, embodied existence of the preacher, the congregation, and the world in which preacher and congregation live. God chooses most to be revealed in preaching not when the preacher strives to become invisible, a hollow tube through which the Word comes, but when she is most present in her particular, embodied humanity, meeting the text and God in the text.

In relation to the comment, "they didn't come here to see you," this incarnational argument leads to the position that it is true in an ultimate sense that the congregation hopes to meet God through the preacher's sermon, but it is also true that they are in some sense there to see the preacher, to see God through the preacher. As we noted above, the sermon is the most personal element of the worship service. While all elements of the liturgy aim to reveal God, the sermon aims to bring about this meeting with God precisely *through* an encounter with the person preaching. The role of the sermon in the liturgy is to be the place where the personal is brought in most strongly as a valid medium through which God speaks. When this is done well, it manifests to hearers that their own personhood and personal existence are likewise vehicles for God's revelation, just as the preacher's personhood is. Their own personal existence is included as an arena of God's revelation.

However, taking Barth's cautions to heart, and absorbing the wisdom of the comment, "they didn't come here to see you," it is important that this personal element in preaching be present in a way that enhances rather than detracts from the ultimate goal of encountering God. Given that the sermon is an event that is strongly inflected by the personal, how can this personal element be incorporated into the sermon in such a way that it does not become an obstruction to God's revelation? I propose that the theory and practice of performance can provide a helpful framework for answering this question, since performance involves negotiating a similarly tensive relationship between a performing self and another. Disciplines of performance can help preachers understand the place of the personal in a suitably nuanced way, so that they can in practice bring this personal element to the sermon in such a way that it enhances the revelatory event taking place.

PERFORMANCE THEORY AND THE SELF-OTHER RELATIONSHIP

The idea that "performance" is a useful metaphor for a preacher's practice requires unpacking the meaning of this word, since in relationship to preaching, the term "performance" has had mostly negative connotations. If we come away from a sermon saying, "It felt like a performance," this is of course a negative judgment on the event. Performance in this usage means a deception, something artificial, something that covers up rather than reveals the truth of text and preacher. If we explore the nuances of this term, however, especially as it has been used both in theology and in many other fields in recent years, the term turns out to contain levels of meaning that prove helpful as a framework for thinking about the role of the personal in preaching.

In recent years the term "performance" has been widely used in many fields in the humanities and social sciences, as well as in theology, so much so that a field of studies called "performance theory" now exists to explore the many meanings and uses of the term. As Marvin Carlson points out, "performance" is a complicated and essentially contested concept; disagreement about its meaning is built into the term itself, such that it is impossible to agree on any single meaning of the term.[5] Carlson notes four clusters of meaning attached to the word "performance." The first draws attention to a public display of particular skills, such as takes place, for instance, in a musical recital. The second cluster of meanings highlights the fact that performance involves behaviors that are consciously separated from the person doing them, so that there is "a certain distance between 'self' and behavior, as for instance the distance between an actor and the role this actor plays on stage." What is significant here is that the behavior that the self engages in

5. Carlson, *Performance*, 1.

is not spontaneously invented by the self, but is rather a repetition of a previously made script. In the case of an actor onstage this is clearly the case, in that the actor performs a character that has been created by another. However, Richard Schechner notes that this kind of behavior goes beyond the stage, and he coins the term "restored behavior" to describe it. As Carlson describes this concept, "restored behavior emphasizes the process of repetition and the continued awareness of some 'original' behavior, however distant or corrupted by myth or memory, which serves as a kind of grounding for the restoration."[6] The idea of "restored behavior" thus describes those actions in which we repeat culturally coded behaviors, with the hope of recapturing the power of an original event. Schechner points out that "restored behavior" takes place not only on stage, but in rituals, trances, shamanism, and psychoanalysis, and elsewhere. The liturgy of the Eucharist is a good example of "restored behavior": through repeating the script of the eucharistic prayer we hope to "restore" or recapture an original event, in this case Jesus's last meal with his disciples.

Closely connected to this idea of restored behavior is, third, the notion that performed actions are those done with a consciousness of their symbolic or signifying potential. An action offstage is merely *done*, but onstage it is *performed*, meaning that it is supposed to mean something; often what it means is connected to a culturally coded behavior that the performer is repeating or restoring. A fourth cluster of meanings for the term "performance" points to the "general success of the activity in light of some standard of achievement." In this sense the word "performance" can be applied to non-human entities, as for instance when we consider the "performance" of an automobile. Significantly, in this fourth meaning of the term, the observer rather than the performer is the one who judges the success of the performance, bringing into focus the fact that performance is always performance *for someone*. This fourth meaning overlaps with the second, in that, when we engage in "restored behavior," repeating a culturally coded pattern of behavior, this culturally coded pattern or original template for behavior is the

---

6. Ibid., 47.

standard according to which others may judge if the performer is enacting the "restored behavior" successfully or not.

Carlson notes one overarching feature of all of these understandings of performance: "all performance involves a consciousness of doubleness, according to which the actual execution of an action is placed in mental comparison with a potential, an ideal, or a remembered original model of that action. Normally this comparison is made by an observer of the action . . . but the double consciousness, not the external observation, is what is most central . . . Performance is always performance *for* someone, some audience that recognizes and validates it as performance even when, as is occasionally the case, that audience is the self."[7] This idea of doubleness encompasses the four meanings of performance just outlined. It encompasses the display of skills, inasmuch as these skills are presented to and assessed by observers. Second, this idea of doubleness points to the distance between self and behavior, in that the performer is attempting to capture an "other," a character, a script, or a culturally sanctioned mode of behavior, that is not the same as the performer himself, and so there is a consciousness of doubleness built into the performer's actions. Third, the idea of doubleness points to the symbolic nature of performance, in which there is on one level an action or practice, and on a deeper level what it symbolizes or means. Finally, the concept of performance as action in light of a standard introduces a consciousness of doubleness in the performer, who is aware that her actions are being compared to an ideal that she may or may not be meeting, and that her actions are displayed to others who will be assessing whether she meets this ideal.

These dimensions of the concept of performance suggest how this concept can describe not only actions taken on a stage but also actions taken in daily life. In daily life we participate in social performance, meaning that we structure our lives according to recognized, repeated, socially sanctioned codes of behavior. These socially structured actions count as "performance" in that they differ from the "self" who does them, and to the extent that

---

7. Ibid., 5.

Preaching and the Personal

we are aware of this, there is a consciousness of doubleness that makes these social behaviors into performance. Moreover, these social performances are almost always enacted for others, such that our actions are displayed rather than merely done, and this feature, too, makes these actions into performances. Finally, inasmuch as we enact these social roles in comparison to a standard, in light of certain recognized cultural codes of behavior, these behaviors count as performance.

It is this notion of daily social and cultural activity as performance that has led theorists like Judith Butler and others to propose that all human activity could be considered as performance. Butler develops philosopher of language J. L. Austin's concept of performative utterance, by which Austin describes forms of language that do not refer to a pre-given reality but rather create the state of affairs which they describe. Butler uses this notion to describe the way that human identity is constituted, particularly focusing on the constitution of gender. Butler argues that gender is not a stable, fixed identity from which acts proceed; rather, gender is an identity constituted through acts, especially the stylized repetition of acts, involving the stylization of the body. The appearance of a stable identity is actually a performative project. The body itself is not a pre-given entity, but is a performance, an act. The ways we perform our bodies, and constitute ourselves as a particular gender, are not unique to ourselves, nor are they only products of our own interiority and creativity; rather, we step into and enact social roles, which precede us. Moreover, as Butler points out, these performances of gender are driven by social taboos. If we do not correctly perform our gender according to culturally recognized and approved patterns of behavior, we are punished; thus the performance of gender is done under duress. Butler's argument about the constitution of gender identity draws on the concept of *habitus* as developed by Pierre Bourdieu. A person's *habitus* emerges from practice, from performing a social role in one's very body, which then comes to shape the body's self-presentation—ways of being, moving, gesturing—becoming in the end a way of life. For Butler and Bourdieu, *habitus* is itself a form of performance, it is "a tacit form of performativity, a citational claim lived and believed at the level of the body."[8] One's total way of life, one's *habitus*, emerges from repeated performance of socially given norms and roles, and is in an implicit sense always a citation or continued performance of those roles, whether one affirms or subverts them. The idea of the self as a performative project also leads to the more general point, commonly made in postmodern thought, that challenges the modern idea of the unified, stable subject, in favor of notions of fragmentary and fluid selves, constituted by performances rather than pre-existing them.

DOUBLENESS IN THE PERFORMANCE TO PREACHING

How do these various notions of performance shed light on the practice of preaching, and specifically on the place of the personal in it? The value of performance theory for our investigation is that it attempts to theorize the relationship between the performing self, the "other" that the self performs, and the audience who witnesses the performance—that is to say, it seeks to understand the personal in relation to its others. In this sense performance theory is applicable to preaching, since preaching too involves a complex relationship between the preacher and various "others"—God, the congregation, and the text of Scripture, among others. Because of these relationships there is a doubleness inherent in the practice of preaching, a distance between self and role, self and God, self and text. Preaching is always "restored behavior," always an attempt to embody an original that is other than the performer (whether this be God or the text which witnesses to God). The element of display, which is embedded in concepts of performance, is central to the event of preaching, which more than almost any other Christian practice is a display of faith before others. The feature of judgment that is inherent in performance appears in preaching as the audience/congregation's attempt to assess how well the preacher is performing this "restoration," that is, how well she is embodying this divine other. The symbolic quality of performance is present in

---

8. Butler, *Excitable Speech*, 155, quoted in Carlson, *Performance*, 79.

preaching as the question of whether the preacher's performance appropriately symbolizes this other, or whether it is symbolizing something else.

The question of the role of the personal in preaching is a question about how to navigate this essential doubleness, this complex relationship between self and others in preaching. The place of the personal in preaching becomes problematic when the inevitable doubleness in preaching opens up into a gap between the preacher and the other she is performing—that is, when there is a sense of the distance between the personal (the preacher's own personhood, capacities and limitations) and the God whose word she is seeking to proclaim and embody. When this happens, then the personal, detached from the role it is supposed to be playing, becomes obtrusive, as Barth puts it. This is when it is necessary to issue the admonition, "remember, they did not come here to see you."

The counsel of Barth, and the thrust of this admonition, is to cope with this doubleness by minimizing the role of the personal as much as possible in preaching. However, the theory of doubleness, as explored in performance theory, suggests a more dialectical solution to this problem, one in which the preacher manifests the other precisely through her full presence in the preaching event. It is an axiom in many schools of acting, for instance, that the actor cannot truthfully portray a character until he discovers his own authentic relationship to that character. Actors, in other words, bring the fullness of themselves—their particularity, life experience, and perspective—to the roles they are playing, and it is only in doing so that they play their characters faithfully.

It is this dialectical relationship—the simultaneous presence of self and other—that Rowan Williams elucidates when he describes the incarnation of the Word of God using the metaphor of performance. Williams employs the idea of performance to describe the relationship between the eternal Son of God or Word of God (the second person of the Trinity), and the human Jesus of Nazareth—that is, the relationship between Jesus Christ's divinity and his humanity. Williams explores the idea of performance by noting that a performer's task is to bring to life the work of another. Here is the idea of doubleness, the relationship between the performing self and that which is performed. Williams argues that in this enactment the performer remains herself, and yet is completely taken up by the work and vision and even selfhood of another:

> Here is someone who is completely themselves (sic), free and independent, and yet for this time the whole of their being, their life, their freedom, their skill, is taken up with this mysterious, different thing that is the work to be brought to life. The vision and imagination of another person, the composer, has to come through—not displacing the human particularity of the performer but 'saturating' that performer's being for the time of the performance.[9]

The human Jesus, Williams argues, is a performer in this way; he is performing God's love and God's purpose, and performs them perfectly, "yet he is never other than himself, with all that makes him distinctly human taken up with this creative work." His is "a human will and a human life whose power and joy is the performance of who God is and what God wants, the performance of the Word of God." As a performer of God's Word, Jesus is "saturated," through and through, with God's life, and yet, paradoxically, his humanity is most full and real in that performance, because all of his particularity is taken up into and displayed in that performance. Jesus of Nazareth becomes most himself by performing God most fully; his human personhood is most fully manifest in this performance.

Williams draws on several of the meanings embedded in the concept of performance in his use of the term. He draws on the idea that performance involves doubleness, in that the performer, Jesus, is enacting a pattern of actions of an "other," the divine Word of God. This pattern of actions also functions as a standard or ideal that the performer, in this case the human Jesus of Nazareth, strives to meet. Here Williams employs the understanding of performance as action in light of a standard. There is also a hint of Butler's insight here, that we become the selves we are through the performance of certain acts. The identity of the human Jesus of Nazareth is nothing other than his lifelong performance of the Word of God; in the

---

9. R. Williams, *Tokens of Trust*, 74.

performance of this Word he also *is* this Word. What is striking in Williams's formulation of Jesus as performer of the Word of God is that in this performance the dialectic between the performing self (the human Jesus) and the other performed (the divine Word of God) is no longer experienced as a conflict or a gap, but becomes the true expression of each party. What disappears in Jesus's performance of the Word of God is the consciousness of doubleness, the awareness that one is playing the part of another; rather, in this performance self and other saturate each other without remainder. The personal is fully present, yet in this very presence the divine other is also made manifest.

Williams's use of the metaphor of performance suggests the value of this metaphor for understanding the role of the personal in preaching. The metaphor of performance, as explicated by Williams, suggests that it is when the personal is most present *in a certain way* that the sermon becomes open to divine revelation. As the preacher brings her personhood to the preaching event, as she chooses to be most present in her full, embodied, particular humanity, she becomes paradoxically most open for God to reveal Godself through her being and her words. Relying on Williams, we can trace the truth of this paradox back to the incarnation itself. As we have seen, Barth insisted that preaching is modeled after the incarnation, and derives its revelatory power from this event. However, Barth derives from the incarnation a model of the preacher as a transparent window or hollow tube through which the Word comes, uninflected by the preacher's selfhood. If Williams's description of the incarnation, shaped by the metaphor of performance, were used as the model for preaching, this model would suggest that, just as Jesus brings the fullness of his personal humanity to performing the Word of God, so too the preacher would need to bring her own personal selfhood to the event in order for it to be revelatory and authoritative.

Williams's use of the trope of performance suggests that the doubleness inherent in preaching, the distance between self and text, self and God, need not lead to a distorted or inappropriate role for the personal. Rather, in the incarnation it is precisely in being his fully human self that Jesus is "saturated" by God, and in this saturation Jesus becomes the fullness of his human self. The metaphor of saturation is helpful here, because a saturated object (like a sponge) still retains its basic shape, but is clearly full of something foreign to it (water). Williams's theology of performance shows how divinity and humanity can be related in the event of preaching, in such a way that saturating humanity with divinity is at the same time an honoring of humanity in its particular and personal shape. The trope of performance suggests that it is *necessary* for the preacher to bring her personhood fully to the preaching event, and only thus is God also fully present. The concept of performance elucidates why it is that the preacher's personal presence is a necessary part of the inspiration of preaching.

The problem with applying Williams's performative understanding of the incarnation to the practice of preaching is that there is a vast difference between the performance of God's Word that Jesus of Nazareth is able to perform, and the performance of that Word that imperfect preachers can perform. Even though we are called to imitate Christ in our preaching as in all things, there is still a distance between what we are capable of and what he is capable of. This then becomes a practical problem, namely, how are we to accomplish this performance of God's Word given all of our imperfections, and to do so in such a way that this performance does not emphasize the personal and its imperfection in ways that are obtrusive or distracting? Although Williams's doctrine of the incarnation shows us an ideal relationship between the personal and its others in preaching, how are we to attain this ideal?

Stanley Hauerwas's use of the concept of performance to describe the dynamics of the Christian life takes us partway to an answer to this question. Hauerwas argues that the Christian faith is primarily neither subjective experience nor an objective deposit of content, but is rather a performance, a set of actions.[10] He gravitates to the term "performance" because he argues that it provides a place for human creativity and initiative, yet takes place within a set of rules, which in this case are those provided by the Christian tradition. Here again, as with Williams, it is the idea of doubleness

---

10. Hauerwas, *Performing the Faith*, 76.

or "restored behavior," behavior that copies a socially coded and sanctioned pattern, that draws Hauerwas to performance as a useful descriptor of the Christian life. In this case the code followed is the pattern for the Christian life. The concept of performance also highlights the quality of display, being done for others, which is part of Hauerwas's conception of the Christian life. He points out that the intelligibility and persuasiveness of the faith depend not on independently formulated criteria but on convincing performances of the faith in people's lives. That is, a convincing performance of the faith on the part of a Christian can make others believe in the truth of the faith. Inherent in this idea is the notion that Christian faith is not simply lived, but also performed, in the sense of being on display to others in order to change them.

Embedded in Hauerwas's use of the trope of performance is the dialectical relationship between the performer and that which is performed, in this case the Christian faith. Hauerwas draws on the idea that there is a doubleness that marks all performances, but he argues that the purpose of repeated performance is so that this relationship of doubleness might change over time. Like Williams, Hauerwas argues that performance of the faith makes the performer (the Christian) more fully herself *precisely as* she embodies the script that is outside of her (in this case the Christian faith). In this performance, the performer is, as Hauerwas describes it, "drawn out of him- or herself and is 'possessed' or 'taken over' by the work . . . In this sense, true performance takes us out of ourselves (*ekstasis*), only to return us to ourselves fuller, richer, more deeply changed."[11] Thus Hauerwas maintains that "good performers of the Christian faith, like good musicians, are those who have refined the art of allowing themselves to be played by the work even as they perform it," in other words to letting their lives express the Christian faith. Hauerwas also insists on the importance of this performance unfolding in time, such that the performance of the faith is not a one-time occasion, but is a pattern of actions that ultimately transforms the performer. Thus Hauerwas, not unlike Butler, sees performance as a vehicle for the transformation of the self; the self

---

11. Ibid., 101.

becomes something that it was not before, by means of performing a pattern of behavior that precedes the self. More than Williams, Hauerwas emphasizes the way that repeated performance of the Christian life transforms a person over time into the *habitus* of a true Christian. Jesus of Nazareth, performing the Word of God, did not need to be transformed into holiness, because he already had this quality in perfection. Human beings, however, need to be and are transformed by their performance of the faith over time.

The use that Hauerwas makes of the concept of performance is helpful for preachers in part because it suggests how preachers are transformed, how the personal is transformed, through undertaking this preaching practice over time. Using Hauerwas, we might say that the personal needs to be present in preaching precisely so that in this repeated performance it can be transformed into a "fuller, richer" holier version of itself. It is essential that the personal be drawn into the preaching event, precisely so that it can be transformed in the encounter with God that preaching aims to create. As Hauerwas's theory of performance indicates, the personal is necessary in preaching precisely because the transformation of the personal, in the person of the preacher, becomes a display or model for listeners to enable their own transformations. If the personal were absent from preaching, one would not witness the embodiment of Christian truth and how this truth can change a life. The personal is necessary in preaching because it demonstrates, in an exemplary fashion, how the personal itself is transformed when brought into encounter with God.

For this reason we can think of the doubleness we experience in preaching not as alienating but as redemptive. In preaching we are given a "script" to perform, which is that of the eschatologically perfected person that God calls us to become. Currently, in our not fully perfected state, there is a doubleness, a gap between the self we are now and this script. This gap is painful at times to inhabit, but this doubleness can also be freeing, because in being given this script we are given a part to play that is the part for which we were created, the part we long to play. This is how preaching can be redemptive for the preacher—taking on this role is the way to become truer to ourselves than we could ever imagine being prior to taking on the role. A preacher once said to me, "I believe things when I am preaching that I do not believe at any other time." This is not a confession of hypocrisy; this is a confession about the power of preaching to transform us, to make us into vessels for God's Word who in that preaching moment, actually, proleptically, show forth the eschatologically perfected selves we will become when we have grown into the full stature of that Word.

To say that preaching is an eschatological event, a glimpse into God's kingdom, is another way of saying that preaching is sacramental. The sacraments are fundamentally eschatological events, in which the Holy Spirit comes upon the elements to make them revelatory of God, to lift them not so much *up* to God (contra Calvin) as *forward* into God's realized kingdom. We get a proleptic glimpse of that kingdom in the breaking of the bread and the moment of eating and drinking together, for the promise is there in the Eucharistic prayer that this is but a foretaste of God's heavenly banquet. So too one might say that in preaching the Holy Spirit breathes in the preacher and carries her forward into her eschatologically realized self—changed from glory into glory, before our eyes—and this display to the hearers is more than a spectator event, for we are all carried forward with her to a place where we not only say but also believe and even know the truths of faith. When this happens the doubleness the preacher inhabits in preaching becomes redemptive rather than destructive.

THE DISRUPTIVE PERSONAL BODY AND THE ESCHATOLOGICAL SELF

The personal needs to be present in preaching in order that it may participate in and display to others a process of transformation through the encounter with God the other, which leads ultimately toward the vanishing point of Jesus Christ's perfect performance of the Word of God, and toward our own eschatological fulfillment. This necessary presence of the personal, however, still leaves us with the question of *how* the personal can be engaged in preaching in ways that lead toward this transformation into holiness. The resources of performance theory suggest a dialectical or paradoxical answer to this question, namely, that we do not arrive at these perfect performances *unless* the personal, even or especially in its very disruptiveness and unruliness, is allowed to be manifest in the performance. The fact that the personal is a disruptive element in performance is suggested by the fact of doubleness itself. Because of doubleness, because there is a gap between the performer and that which is performed, there is always a remainder or excess in the performer's performance of the role, script, or character. There is always something of the personal that seems to fall outside the perfect performance, not to fit the performance. Butler makes this argument when she discusses the performance of gender norms, noting in effect that there is inevitably a sort of slippage or wiggle room in our performance of these norms, simply because they are a performance. She notes that since the ground of gender identity is a stylized repetition of acts, not a pre-given and seamless identity, there are possibilities for gender transformation, for challenging and subverting these culturally given codes; these possibilities for transformation are found in how we repeat or change these acts, these performances.[12] Moreover, performance brings us into our bodies; it is the creation of *habitus* at the bodily level, and Butler notes that the body is never contained by its performance of social norms, but always produces an excess that undermines the norms it performs. There is always a slippage between the original social role and our repetition of it, and this slippage, importantly, has to do with the body's involvement, its unruliness in relation to all norms.

We can note the ways in which this slippage, introduced by the body's presence, complicates the performance of the other in preaching. For instance, the presence of the preacher's body means that aspects of her personhood carry symbolic power beyond what her words themselves communicate, and beyond what she can fully control or direct. The preacher's body language, bearing and demeanor symbolize things of which the preacher is not always conscious, and thus cannot fully control. Moreover, the preacher's social location is visible in her body, in terms of race, gender, and

---

12. Butler, "Performative Acts and Gender Constitution," 120–34.

class, and this can make preachers feel powerless about what they may be communicating through their very presence, beyond their conscious intention. The body disrupts perfect performances of the Word also because it is subject to various physical processes that cannot be fully socially controlled. We may feel the disruptiveness of the body in preaching as a sense that our physical presence is at odds with our conscious purpose—for instance, when our voices are too soft to be heard, when we do not know what to do with our hands, when we do not know where to rest our eyes. Underneath these discomforts is a deeper unease with the body itself, in part because of the body's inevitable association with sex and death, two unruly and uncontrollable aspects of human experience. It is intriguing to note how certain aspects of the choreography of preaching conspire to deal with this discomfort by hiding the body in various ways—dressing it up in robes that conceal the particulars of the preacher's body, or positioning it behind pulpits that conceal most of the body below the head (making it look like the idea of the human person we are most comfortable with—the person as disembodied mind or spirit, a head only). It may even be that the disruptive, embarrassing, not fully controllable presence of the body in preaching is the nodal point for the concerns about the presence of the personal in preaching; all of these concerns actually originate in a sense of embarrassment about the body, that which is most personal in preaching.

For Butler and other performance theorists, however, the disruptions of perfect performance caused by the body and its unruliness are not troubling but instead create space for liberation from restrictive performances. Here Butler is joining a debate within performance theory about whether performance is essentially conservative or subversive. Do performers enact culturally coded behaviors so as to reinforce them and to curtail deviation from them, or can performers enact these behaviors so as to subvert and transform them? Butler argues that performance contains the possibility of transgression of constraining performances, thus creating space to allow new identities to form in contrast to those identities imposed by cultural norms. It is the body's disruptive excess that disrupts every performance, thus creating the possibility for these transgressions and for new expressions of identity to arise.

This possibility suggests that the disruptiveness of the personal, and especially the preacher's personal body, needs to be included in order for preaching to fulfill its transformative potential. The presence of the personal and especially the body may seem like an intrusion into the performance of the Word of God, but can actually lead toward the fulfillment of that performance on a deeper level. One reason why this is so is that the unruliness of the personal and the body, when invited into preaching, can disturb notions of the human self as shaped into the Christian *habitus* that may be too conventional. Our understandings of what it means to be the people of God may be too shaped by secular cultural norms, and perhaps only through the discomfiting presence of the body can we find our way to a truer performance of this citizenship. Christian identity may be something far more radical and transgressive than we can now descry, but it may be embedded proleptically in the body and its wisdom.

Sarah Coakley advances one portrayal of the way in which the Christian identity, in its eschatological fulfillment, radically subverts cultural norms. Coakley uses Butler's notion of gender as a performative project to argue that the goal of this project, from a Christian perspective, is a self freed of gender constraint. Coakley finds this end described in the eschatological vision of the self found in Gregory of Nyssa, among other Christian theologians.[13] In Nyssen's ascetical theology she finds "forms of gender fluidity and reversal . . . that undercut and subvert what could be expected of someone living according to the late-antique norms of married gender roles."[14] Coakley extends Gregory's "eschatologically-oriented theory of gender," to argue that a condition of gender fluidity will be the human condition fully realized at the eschaton, and it is that condition toward which all performances of gender transgression are oriented.

---

13. Coakley, *Powers and Submissions*, 157.
14. Ibid., 164.

Preaching and the Personal

According to Coakley, therefore, under the multiple performances of the self that Butler describes, there is a true self, which is the eschatologically realized person of faith. As an *eschatological* self, this true self is not in our possession now, but it is an identity we can perform our way into, not by performing a societally given script of gender (or other) norms, but by performing our Christian faith. Coakley and Hauerwas would agree with Butler that the self is a performative project: we become the selves we are through performance of a script that is given us. But when that script is the Christian faith, then Coakley and Hauerwas argue that performing this script makes us our true, authentic selves. In effect, while some performance theorists argue for a "strategic essentialism" that allows for the forming of alternative identities in contrast to culturally enforced identities, Coakley is arguing for an "eschatological essentialism" that allows for the formation of the people of God in contrast to secularly enforced identities.

However, if it is true that the eschatologically realized Christian is a person in whom gender is fluid, then the performances of that identity which we enact in order to be shaped into this *habitus* will undoubtedly be disruptive of current cultural norms in which, as Butler emphasizes, gender performances are enforced under strict taboos. This is but one example of ways in which the performance of Christian identity is subversive of secular norms of human personhood. If preaching is an exemplary performance of Christian identity, through which that identity is transformed, then this performance needs to allow space for the disruptiveness and transgressiveness of the personal and the body, because this identity we are performing our way into is itself transgressive of culturally given norms. There is a riskiness to preaching when the personal is present in this way, but it is the riskiness that upends norms in order to birth something new. By allowing the disruptive excess of the body's presence in preaching, we can occupy the wiggle room or place of slippage identified by Butler in her account of performance, and this can allow for a subversion of pre-determined norms and the birthing of new possibilities for Christian identity.

The presence of the personal and the body both troubles preaching and is essential to its fulfillment as a performance that shapes both preacher and hearers into their true Christian identity. The reason for this is ultimately a theological one: the personal body of the preacher is the site where the Holy Spirit enters our lives and transforms us. The Holy Spirit is the breath, the *ruach*, of God. The breath entering and leaving our bodies is, quite literally, the Spirit inhabiting, enlivening, and transforming us. One point of awareness I teach my students is that, when they stand in alignment and allow their breathing muscles to relax, the breath *happens to* them, rather than their making it happen. Instead of breathing, we *are breathed*. In a concrete, intimate, and immediate way, we sense the presence and agency of God in our bodies.

It is this divine presence, this divine breath of the Holy Spirit, which disrupts everything. This Spirit-breath within us produces the excess that undermines and defies social norms, upending our carefully calibrated performances of them. I see this unsettling presence of the Spirit regularly in my work teaching preaching. When preaching students allow breath to drop into their bodies and to connect with the truths they know and the feelings they feel, they find themselves speaking astonishing truths, truths they did not previously know were there. They may come to class with a prepared sermon, but when they allow the breath to infuse the words, very often the words change to something truer, deeper, more raw, less conventional.

The same disruptive presence of the Spirit is apparent when students undertake the practice of learning and performing biblical texts. To "perform" a text means to take it several steps beyond reciting it or reading it out loud. It is to take on the voices of the characters, to stage the text, to decide what the scene looks like. It is to portray the text as an event or tell it as a story. But in order to do this, a central principle of acting must be observed, which is that the truth of the text emerges not when the performer effaces herself in relation to the text, as Barth urges, but when she enters into active relationship with it, when she brings the personal—her body, voice, and life experience—to bear upon the text. The hermeneutic of performance is one in which truth emerges out of a conversation between performer and text.

Preaching and the Personal

When students engage in this process, when they allow breath, feeling, and personal experience to come to the words of scripture, the words become destabilizing, excessive, impossible to contain within culturally bounded norms. Students are often shocked to discover the iconoclastic force of scripture, once they allow their bodies to fully know these sacred words and what they mean. Students discover, in other words, how these sacred words are channels that connect them to God's presence, will, and desire. Talal Asad comments that the inability "to enter into communion with God" may well be "a function of untaught bodies."[15] What these performance practices are essentially doing is teaching bodies how to be in relationship with God, by teaching them how to be open to Holy Spirit, and Spirit-inspired Word. In the process what happens is that the disruptiveness of the personal is infused by the disruptiveness of the Spirit, so that the personal can continue to be transformed into the identity of the people of God.

There is no question that to allow the personal into preaching in this way creates a danger and a risk. It is common to argue that the danger of the personal in preaching is that it becomes the focus, seizing the spotlight and occluding the presence of God the other. But the deeper danger is that in allowing the personal into preaching, as the place that the Spirit breathes into and transforms, we create the possibility for performances that transgress and disrupt established norms so that a new identity can be shaped within us. We can foreclose that possibility by warning, "they did not come here to see you," but may in so doing close down the possibility for the Spirit to breathe within us and transform us. By contrast, if we allow our personal bodies to be present in preaching, and to be available to the Spirit and its dangerous truths, we may well discover ourselves being transformed into selves of greater joy, delight, and faithfulness than we can now imagine. Through the presence of the personal in this way, preachers allow themselves to be vessels for the fulfillment of preaching's ultimate purpose, which is a transformative encounter with God. Preachers will never enact perfectly the incarnational performance of Jesus Christ, in which human and

---

15. Asad, "Remarks on the Anthropology of the Body," 48.

divine are both fully manifest, but as we offer the personal, and then allow it to be transformed through the performance of this other (the text, and God in the text), we become our essential selves and at the same time are inspired by the divine breath and participate in the becoming flesh of the divine Word.

4

The Risk of Testimony

WALTER BRUEGGEMANN

In 1977, Elie Wiesel notably wrote,

> If the Greeks invented tragedy, the Romans the epistle, and the Renaissance the sonnet, our generation invented a new literature, that of testimony.[1]

In a contribution to a volume titled *Dimensions of Holocaust*, Wiesel refers specifically to the death-camp survivors who are the surviving witnesses and testifiers to a truth that might otherwise be ignored and forgotten and, in some quarters, vigorously denied. Of course, Wiesel, for obvious reasons, overstates the case of new twentieth-century inventiveness. He wants to insist that the entire reality of the death camps is without precedent or parallel. Given that, the consequent act of testimony from the death-camps is derivatively also without precedence or parallel. That of course is not factually true; the truth rather is that folk in pain have been forever speaking their truth against the establishment, at least since the

---

1. Wiesel, "The Holocaust as Literary Inspiration," 9.

slaves in Egypt groaned and cried out when pharaoh died (Exod 2:23–25).

THE OFFER OF TESTIMONY

We may therefore take Wiesel's clue to the character of testimony without his historical claim and consider the recurring circumstance of testimony, the emergence of testimony, the truth it carries, and the risk it necessarily entails. At the outset we recognize that "testimony" rings the cadences of a juridical context, as I have argued in my *Theology of the Old Testament*.[2] Witnesses—testifiers, martyrs—appear regularly before the bar of judgment, a bar variously consisting in demanding interrogators, the court of public opinion, or the long term judgment of history. They do so in order to voice an advocacy about how events are to be understood and eventually about the particular world that has been observed and experienced. I propose that these five elements belong to the offer of testimony and the proposal of truth:

1. Testimony emerges or *erupts in a world of silence*, often a context of enforced silence in which establishment power controls the conversation and does not want the conversation to continue. The enforcer of silence may be variously the empire—because empires survive on the basis of silence—or totalizing coercion in the church, community, or family that is variously authorized by age, race, gender, or other valued social distinctions. Such domination at micro or macro level invites no "voice from below" and, if possible, permits none.

2. The emerging, erupting witness *refuses the silence. It breaks the silence* and offers utterance that contradicts the claims of the dominator. We have seen many such occasions of bold persons and movements in our own contemporary context who have run great risks in breaking silence and who characteristically bring down on themselves the wrath of the silencer. Such breaking of silence is propelled, characteristically, by the reality of pain and suffering, by a dignity that refuses to give

2. Brueggemann, *Theology of the Old Testament*, 117–22.

in, and by a profound hope that it need not be so.

3. The very utterance of such pain, dignity, and hope in a context that generates pain, overrides dignity, and nullifies hope *puts establishment truth in contestation*. Until there is such testimony, the truth of the dominant system remains uncontested and nobody dare entertain the thought that it could be otherwise. But once uttered, the supremacy and immunity of establishment truth is placed in irreversible jeopardy, and eventually negotiation and adjudication must be undertaken in order to find a new arrangement of power and a new articulation of truth.[3]

4. The witnesses do not get to decide the outcome of such articulation and such adjudication. Rather they set in motion processes that run well beyond their own utterance. Their work is to break the silence, to mount a contest, and to insist upon openness to a possibility not heretofore entertained. That *insistence upon openness* will be marked by honesty about pain, nerve about dignity, and resilience about hope.

5. Whereas establishment truth has much credentialing and authorization on its side, most often establishment logic, academic support, data and footnotes, the witness characteristically *only has a story to tell*, and perhaps *bodily scars* that bespeak both pain and hope. The wonder of such testimony is that it offers a sub-version of reality that subverts established truth. The utterance and its hearing reach below managed explanation and have the chance of human-touch-to-human, in order to effect transformation of vision and practice that the establishment can no longer preclude. (It follows, in my rendition, that such witness is never an utterance of establishment truth; no witnesses are needed for that.)

Thus, in Wiesel's case, in which testimony is "invented," there was for a long time a silence about the death camps with many

---

3. For a novelistic presentation of the way in which utterance creates historical possibility, see Brink, *A Chain of Voices*.

respected colluders.[4] There has been the breaking of the silence, though it required a generation for the voices from below to form effective ways; there was a challenge to preferred establishment truth, a "new truth" of pain, dignity, and hope. This new truth is a human-touch-to-human, and an inevitable, required renegotiation of how truth will be uttered among us concerning that brutality.

DEUTERO-ISAIAH

We may, however, go behind the contemporary reality of such testimony. In the Christian Old Testament / the Hebrew Bible, the most dramatic usage of testimony is in Deutero-Isaiah, in the midst of exile. (In the New Testament, the parallel is found in the Fourth Gospel, on which see Andrew Lincoln.)[5] The poetry of Deutero-Isaiah reflects the utterance of the Jewish community in the midst of Babylonian hegemony. That hegemony had, for all practical purposes, silenced Jewish hope and eliminated Jewish historical possibility. It was clear that the Babylonian gods had triumphed over YHWH and had legitimated raw imperial power. To some extent, the silencing of Jewish historical possibility was coercive and heavy-handed; but it surely was also the case that the silencing was accomplished by seduction, as some Jews surely colluded with Babylonian power in order to make it in the Babylonian economy. The empire was vigorously totalizing and did not allow thought or utterance or gesture outside that totality.[6] (We have witnessed such totalizing capacity in the twentieth century; in many quarters, moreover, the church has proceeded by a totaling of its own).[7]

But then, in ways that we do not understand, the silence is broken. The poet in Deutero-Isaiah broke the silence in daring, lyrical ways that contest the truth of Babylonian claims. The silence

---

4. See Wiesel, *The Jews of Silence*.
5. Lincoln, *Truth on Trial*.
6. I take my cue from Levinas, *Totality and Infinity*.

7. It is not unimportant that the familiar adage, "Power corrupts and absolute power corrupts absolutely," was coined during the process through which the Roman Catholic hierarchy arrived at "papal infallibility" in 1870.

is broken, says the poet, by the instigation of the holy God who finally will not be dismissed, but who authorized this speaker to "get you up on a high mountain" (Isa 40:9). This poet three times uses the term "gospel" in a theological way never before employed in ancient Israel. His "testimony" is "news" that breaks the silent totality of Babylon by an "experience" (so he claims) of being present in the council of the gods from which poetry is generated (Isa 40:1–11). In his claim, he of course replicates Isaiah of Jerusalem who in chapter 6 "experienced" a vision of God surrounded by God's heavenly acolytes.[8]

From that "experience" the poet bears witness to Jews that an alternative to the empire is possible, that life outside the empire is livable, but that it will require a willful, risky departure from empire. The veracity of his defiant utterance, in which he calls other Jews to risk, is based only in his hidden experience to which no one else has access. From that "experience" comes the threefold utterance of the "Gospel":

Get you up on to a high mountain, O Zion, herald of *good tidings;*

> Lift up your voice with strength,
> O Jerusalem, herald of *good tidings,*
> Lift it up, do not fear;
> Say to the cities of Judah,
> "Here is your God." (Isa 40:9)

I first have declared it to you,

> And I give to Jerusalem a herald of *good tidings* (Isa 41:27).

> How beautiful upon the mountains
> Are the feet of the messenger who announces peace,
> Who brings *good news,*
> Who announces salvation,
> Who says to Zion, "Your God reigns." (Isa 52:7)

---

8. On the relation between the two texts, see Seitz, *Zion's Final Destiny,* 36–39, 197–99.

The testimony, rooted in hidden experience, yields an articulation of the power and reality of God amid empire:

> "Here is your God."

> "Our God reigns."

In this utterance based on hidden experience, the poet as witness opens up a large, lyrical alternative world in which Jews are invited to recover enough of their identity in order to act, according to their destiny, against the will of the empire. The sequence of *hidden experience, poetic utterance,* and *engagement in contestation* with imperial truth becomes paradigmatic for Israel's faith, replicated by Jesus before Pilate and by the Apostles in the Book of Acts. Everything depends upon the poet.[9]

But then, remarkably and unexpectedly, the poet as witness recruits his addressees to join the practice of testimony. He imagines a trial in which truth is contested. (All good poetry, I propose, is a contestation between the good news and the deathly option of silencing hegemony.) In Isa 43:8–13,

—The poet mocks the empire by inviting the empire to dispatch witnesses to the trial to make a case for the empire:

> Let them bring their witnesses to justify them,
> And let them hear and say, "It is true." (v. 9)

—The poet summons his Jewish audience:

> You are my witnesses, say the LORD,
> And my servant whom I have chosen. (v. 10)

—The purpose of the recital, it turns out, is not to persuade the Babylonians, but that the Jews themselves would take themselves, by their own poetry, into an alternative future:

> . . . so that you may know and believe me
> And understand that I am he. (v. 10)

---

9. On this proposition, see Brueggemann, *Finally Comes the Poet.*

Preaching and the Personal

—The poet has YHWH give the witnesses their testimony, what they are to say on behalf of YHWH, the new truth that yields a new reality in the world:

> Before me no god was formed,
> Nor shall there be any after me.
> I, I am the LORD,
> And besides me there is no savior.
> I declared and saved and proclaimed,
> When there was no strange god among you. (vv. 10–12)

—After such a lyrical self-announcement for YHWH on the lips of the witnesses, the mandate is reiterated:

> You are my witnesses, says the LORD. (v. 12)

—The poetry culminates in the self-doxology of YHWH that will give the witnesses energy and courage:

> I am God and also henceforth I am He;
> there is no one who can deliver from my hand;
> I work and who can hinder it?

The poem moves between *recruitment of witnesses* and the *substance of their testimony*. For those who believe the testimony (and preserve the poetry), a new world comes into being in the moment of utterance.

DYNAMIC ANALOGY

There is no direct or obvious move from that ancient utterance to our contemporary utterance. But the preacher makes such a move intuitively in what James Sanders calls "dynamic analogy."[10] I propose, in rather simplistic fashion, to suggest that, as Deutero-Isaiah and his recruited witnesses contested Babylonian truth on behalf of the God who is the subject of this poetry, *mutatis mutandis*, the current contestation of truth in the US church is between the ideology of the National Security State that I have elsewhere termed

10. Sanders, *From Sacred Story to Sacred Text*, 70.

"military consumerism" and the narrative of the Triune God, Father, Son and Spirit that is fleshed in the tale of Jesus. That is of course a huge *mutatis mutandis*. It is, however, a *mutatis mutandis* that must be made and regularly is made if we are to attend to *experience*, to *utterance*, and to *credible contestation*. By making such a connection between ancient text and contemporary context, it is possible that the ancient text can provide warrant for how we are to make our own testimony.

I propose that those who would be witnesses for the Gospel in the US can reflect on the truth of the gospel in our own lives in the context of the totalizing claims of the narrative of the consumer economy that is backed by military force that serves a sense of entitlement rooted in the exceptionalism of being God's most recently chosen people. Of course we do not articulate the crisis so directly; we assume, for the most part, entitlement to our standard of living, our legitimate monopoly of markets and resources, and the nobility of democratic capitalism, without thought about the blow-back on us and on those who depend upon us. I will take that common assumption as a given, though we may quibble about the details and its particular articulation. The important point to recognize is that this totalizing narrative is everywhere operative and assured, even though rarely acknowledged.

That totalizing narrative, like the ancient Babylonian one, presumes to make us safe and happy. The "safe" part is the military security system that depends upon deep waves of anxiety and fear. The proud exhibit of military force, the dazzling array of military technology, the endless exhibit of police patrols, the tightening of the borders, the busy charade of airport security, all attest to a "Dick Cheney" strategy of bottomless fear that is matched by entitlement exceptionalism.

The "happiness" part is the pervasive reach of the advertising game, most especially body care and cosmetics, plus the aura of sports spectacles that offer a public that is endlessly at ease and not inconvenienced. This required public is capable of being constantly entertained, so that critical thought becomes neither necessary nor eventually possible.

Preaching and the Personal

The current ideology of "safety and happiness" is evidently a new version of the old imperial offer of "bread and circuses." The wonder is that no one has to pay for it. It is all free, because taxes are an anathema in response to the offer. I propose, not unlike Deutero-Isaiah in ancient Babylon, that the preacher has to break the silence in the midst of this totalizing narrative upon which not many companions have used much critical energy. The preacher as witness must, perforce:

- Break the silence on which the dominant ideology depends;
- Articulate an alternative that puts the truth of the National Security State in contestation;
- Find grounds of credibility in text and in life;
- Invite to a fresh adjudication of truth and power.

Christian testimony has a few programmatic themes. Paul Tillich says that the work of God's rescue in Jesus Christ is that we have been *emancipated from bondage* or we have been *reconciled from alienation*. Or as my United Church of Christ recites about the work of Christ, ". . .conquering sin and death and reconciling the world to God's self." The preacher has those familiar, jaded categories that she can transpose into "safety and happiness," safety as emancipation and happiness as reconciliation. The preacher cannot get free of the ancient text that provides the categories and discloses the Holy Source of testimonial, poetic freedom. At the same time, of course, the preacher lets the old testimony against the ancient empire become the contemporary testimony against the dominant contemporary ideology, whereby the old, old story becomes the new, new song.

The preacher, out of personal experience and out of wider contemporary experience, has the two tasks, the same two tasks as the ancient poet. On the one hand, the preacher must tell tales of the deep dysfunction and falsehood of the dominant story in order to disclose that the imperial gods are powerless to provide either safety or happiness; these gods, powerless as they are, can neither emancipate nor reconcile. The second, more important task, however, is to give testimony, personal and beyond personal, from contemporary life where the God of the Gospel has issued safety that the world does not expect and has provided happiness that the world thinks is impossible. In our evangelical testimony, it is known that safety comes by entrusting ourselves to the neighbor-making fabric of companionable existence in which we are not abandoned to the vagaries of death. It is known, in our evangelical testimony, that happiness comes by the participation in a missional life of self-giving. Both this entrustment of self to the neighborly fabric that yields safety and participation in a missional life of self-giving that offers happiness are profoundly counter-cultural and counter-imperial. The utterance of such testimony is, for that reason, a disruptive contestation whereby the congregation is summoned to negotiate between this new truth and the old, jaded truth of empire that daily summons us and surrounds us.

I have no doubt that personal testimony and other contemporary testimony are important in the preaching task. But with these caveats:

- Such testimony is not primarily designed to be cute or entertaining or trivial, because it mediates a life-or-death contest;
- Such testimony can be too closely personal and, very soon, not interesting or compelling; it needs, rather, to draw personal testimony from others in the awareness that the truth of pain and the reality of hope are often more palpable on lips other than our own.
- Such testimony can be excessively privatized and personalized until the deep, implied ideological contestation in the utterance is played out.
- Such testimony is not "illustration," but is a venue for the redescription of the truth of the world.

When these caveats are honored, I have no doubt that experience-rooted testimony carries enormous authority and transformative creditability in shaking the foundations and opening new futures.

Preaching and the Personal

The gospel of Mark is a model for linking main claims to personal testimony. In Mark 1:14–15, there is a programmatic declaration of the gospel that echoes Deutero-Isaiah:

> Now after John was arrested, Jesus came to Galilee, proclaiming the good news of God, and saying, "The time is fulfilled, and the kingdom of God has come near; repent, and believe in the good news."

This declaration is immediately followed in Mark by concrete narratives of testimony about transformations . . . an unclean spirit, a cleansed leper, a healed paralytic. It is telling that in Mark 2:6 and 3:6, the concrete gospel acts about which testimony is made immediately evoke opposition from the hegemonic company:

> Now some of the scribes were sitting there, questioning in their hearts, "Why does this fellow speak in this way? It is blasphemy! Who can forgive sins but God alone?" (Mark 2:6)

> The Pharisees went out and immediately conspired with the Herodians against him, how to destroy him. (Mark 3:6)

It was not the grand claim that got Jesus in trouble. It was concrete testimony that evoked lethal opposition. Such personal testimony that subverts is urgent in our preaching.

DO NOT FEAR

I finish with one more text. When we genuinely understand testimony as narrated truth that subverts dominant, settled truth, testimony is seen to be serious, risky business. So it was in the ancient world. Quite clearly Jews in Babylon quaked at telling an alternative truth. The poet has God say to Israel as witness:

> Do not fear, or be afraid;
> > have I not told you from of old and declared it?
> > You are my witnesses!

> Is there any god besides me?
> There is no other rock; I know not one. (Isa 44:8)

The juxtaposition of "You are my witnesses" and "Do not fear" constitutes an awareness that witnesses can be frightened in their contestation with settled truth. I can think of two such scenarios:

- A corporate whistleblower, at the last minute, cringes from courtroom testimony because it is too risky; she might lose her pension or endanger her family. Her attorney must remind her that everything rides on her testimony, and she must have courage.

- A raped woman is about to testify against the rapist; at the last minute she does not want to testify, because it is too shameful and too sordid. Her attorney reminds her that the whole case depends on her experience-rooted truth-telling.

That is how it must have been in ancient Babylon; consequently, God must reassure: "You are my witnesses . . . do not fear." To be a witness to alternative truth is a risky venture. That is why, since that ancient poem, serious witnesses must be surrounded by "Do not fear," an assurance rooted in the steadfastness of the God of all truth. It is this one who finally is the witness. Thus Luke has Jesus say:

> But before all this occurs, they will arrest you and persecute you; they will hand you over to synagogues and prisons, and you will be brought before kings and governors because of my name. This will give you an opportunity to testify. So make up your minds not to prepare your defense in advance; for I will I give you words and a wisdom that none of your opponents will be able to withstand or contradict. You will be betrayed even by parents and brother, by relatives and friends; and they will put some of you to death. You will be hated by all because of my name. But not a hair of your head will perish. By your endurance you will gain your souls. (Luke 21:12–19)

Witnessing can become as jaded, routine, and trivial as every other mode of discourse. Its lively urgency depends upon the recognition of the high stakes of the contestation.

5

Collaborative Preaching and the Bible
Toward a Practical Theology of Memory

JOHN S. MCCLURE

SEVERAL LONG-STANDING SHIFTS IN biblical studies suggest that biblical interpretation is done best in a collaborative way. Fernando Segovia, in *Reading from This Place: Social Location and Biblical Interpretation in the United States*, asserted that reading the Bible should involve "positioned readers, flesh-and-blood persons" who are in "critical dialogue" within a "truly global interaction" regarding the meaning of biblical texts.[1] Daniel Patte, in his book *Ethics of Biblical Interpretation: A Re-evaluation*, argued for a conversation between levels of exegetical practice and for the inclusion of the "ordinary reader" in that conversation.[2] In his book, *Texts under Negotiation: The Bible and Postmodern Imagination*, Walter

---

1. Segovia, *Reading from This Place*, 31.
2. Patte, *Ethics of Biblical Interpretation*, 76–84.

Brueggemann argued that "the practice of Christian interpretation in preaching and liturgy is contextual, local, and pluralistic."[3]

Graduates of seminary and divinity schools who have been exposed to these ideas know that awareness of one's social location and the perspective of others can have tremendous influence on biblical interpretation. They see clearly how contextual and situational perspectives not only influenced the production of ancient texts, but also how these factors influence the way texts are interpreted and understood today. Because of this, many preachers and teachers of the Bible in local congregations are not as eager to be in absolute control of the interpretation process, and are able to be more generous when confronted with "ordinary readings." They are also more concerned to use their critical expertise to demonstrate, enhance, support, and build upon such readings, rather than to disprove and discredit them. At the same time, many of these preachers and teachers are ready to engage, and perhaps even to promote, readings that are marginal within their own communities of faith or that bring significant challenges from beyond the boundaries of the church. They are also more likely to bring multiple levels of exegesis (literary, historical, reader-response, etc.) into sustained conversation toward contextual pastoral decisions, instead of making pastoral interpretation subservient to one exegetical standard.

RECEPTION-ORIENTED HOMILETICS

Over the past few decades, reception-oriented homiletics has mirrored these sea-changes in biblical hermeneutics. Reception studies of preaching investigate the processes and practices involved in receiving and using sermons. These studies promote awareness of common reception patterns, as well as issues of social location, identity, and other markers of difference in homiletical theory. Questions involved in such studies include: What difference do race, ethnicity, and social location make in sermon reception? What are the key individual differences that affect sermon reception? What qualities of a sermon make it more effective? What do listeners do

---

3. Brueggemann, *Texts under Negotiation*, 8–10.

with sermons? What is the role of psychology, especially perception and memory, in sermon reception? What are the purposes of the sermon in the lives of listeners?

Empirical studies of reception have increased in the late twentieth-century especially in the North American and German contexts. Most recently, Ronald Allen and a team of investigators in the United States organized the "Listening to Listeners Project," funded by the Lilly Foundation. This study, which took place between 2000 and 2003, used in-depth interviews with individuals and focus groups, and involved more than two hundred fifty lay persons and more than thirty preachers in twenty-eight Midwestern American congregations. The study yielded four books and many articles analyzing listeners's perceptions of content, feeling, the preacher, and embodiment.[4]

As a result of an intensified awareness of issues of reception, there has been a noted "turn to the listener" in homiletic theory since the late 1970s.[5] In its early form this turn took the shape of inductive sermon methods[6] and some experientially grounded narrative and imaginative approaches to preaching.[7] These homiletic models mirrored, in some ways, Kenneth Burke's rhetoric.[8] Burke advocated "identification" with one's interlocutor and encouraged a shift from "persuasion" to "consubstantiality" as the goal for

---

4. McClure et al., *Listening to Listeners*; Allen. *Hearing the Sermon*; Turner-Sharraz et al., *Believing in Preaching*; Allen and Mulligan, *Make the Word Come Alive*; Allen, "Assessing the Authority of a Sermon," 63–74; Allen, "Is Preaching Caught or Taught?," 137–52; Allen, "What Do Lay People Think God is Doing in the Sermon?," 365–75; Allen, "What Makes Preaching Disciples Preaching?," 28–39; Allen, "Preaching after a Tragedy," 221–32; Allen, "How Do People Listen to Sermons?," 52–5; Allen, "Preaching to Listeners," 7; Allen, "Three Settings on which People Hear Sermons," 1–3; McClure, "The Practice of Sermon Listening," 6–9; Turner-Sharazz, "The 'So What' Factor in the Sermon," 45–58.

5. For a summary of this "turn," see Ottoni-Wilhelm, "New Hermeneutic, New Homiletic, and New Directions," 17–31.

6. Craddock, *As One without Authority*; Meyers, *With Ears to Hear*.

7. Lowry, *The Homiletical Plot*; Steimle et al., *Preaching the Story*; Jenson, *Telling the Story*.

8. Burke, *A Rhetoric of Motives*.

rhetoric. Inductive, narrative, and imagination-centered homiletic theories assumed a humanist theory of subjectivity and made use of existentialist philosophies and theologies grounded in ideas of "common human experience." It was assumed that preachers *could* and *should* identify with sermon listeners and speak *from* and *for* listeners when speaking from the pulpit.

In the latter decades of the twentieth century, deconstructive and hermeneutical philosophies, postcolonial theories, cultural studies, standpoint epistemology, critical race theories, and feminist and womanist theories established strong critiques of ideas of sameness or interchangeability with respect to human subjectivity. Since 1990, homiletic theories of reception have demonstrated an increasing responsiveness to these critiques. Homileticians have inserted the awareness of listener *difference* and *otherness* into homiletical theory in a variety of ways. In essence, they have emphasized the need for preachers to speak *with* listeners as they interpret biblical texts, or read biblical commentaries that take marginalized audiences into account (persons with disabilities, victims of abuse, global perspectives, etc.), before speaking *for/to* anyone.

MEMORY AND THE POSTMODERN CONTEXT

The accent on reader/listener difference in the fields of biblical studies and homiletics, and the resulting concern to consult a broad range of readers of scripture and sermon listeners, have coincided with significant shifts in epistemology and memory in the postmodern context. Many believe that memory is at stake in a postmodern situation. When tradition is dislodged and disputed, reason pulled from its foundations, and the interpretation of sacred texts de-centered, memory becomes a site of contestation at best, and nostalgia at worst. Cultural critics Walter Benjamin and Frederic Jameson both warned that cultural de-centering and technological mediation could foster detachment from the past.[9] According to Jameson:

---

9. Benjamin, *Illuminations*; see Jameson, *Postmodern Culture*, 125.

> the disappearance of a sense of history, the way in which our entire contemporary social system has little by little begun to lose its capacity to retain its own past, has begun to live in a perpetual present and in a perpetual change that obliterates traditions of the kind which all earlier social formations have had in one way or another to preserve."[10]

Robert Hewison notices that, with this detachment from the past, a "heritage industry" arises—fostering costumed re-enactments of history and other simulacra of the past.[11] These consumer-driven, themepark gestures at the past stand in for performed rituals of remembering that might preserve the past while enacting new improvisations based on both its wisdom and its transgressions. Memory becomes theatre, and theatre stands in for genuine *performances* of memory, in which people ritualize the various ways in which memory works, and put memory into action in rituals of interpretation and representation.

RECENT HOMILETICAL MODELS AND MEMORY

Four homiletical models have arisen to respond to the shift accompanying the de-centering of listener identity in homiletical theory. Each model approaches memory differently and seeks to make a contribution to the way that memory among listeners to sermons is negotiated and fashioned.

First, *perspectival homiletics*, or "targeted-audience" models assume that the preacher can only have modest amounts of knowledge regarding many listeners: for instance, the elderly; those who have experienced sexual or domestic violence; differently abled persons; those from other races, cultures, or social locations.[12] Because of this, when preparing sermons preachers must identify problems

---

10. Jameson, *Culture*, 125.

11. Hewison, *The Heritage Industry*.

12. Smith, *Preaching as Weeping, Confession, and Resistance*; Black, *A Healing Homiletic*; Nieman and Rogers, *Preaching to Every Pew*; González and Jiménez, *Púlpito*; Kim, *Preaching to Second Generation Korean Americans*; McClure and Ramsay, *Telling the Truth*.

associated with homiletical hegemony of various types and preach sermons using language and hermeneutical perspectives that will welcome a broader base of listeners into the preaching event. In this model, various forms of *counter-memory* are identified and become the focus of the preacher's work in the pulpit. Different reception experiences invite different, and often radically new approaches to biblical texts and to the past, yielding new perspectives on the past and new insights for the present.

A second model, also concerned with fostering forms of counter-memory, is what might be called *counter-testimonial homiletics*. Lucy Atkinson Rose invites the preacher in a pluralistic context to become a provocateur whose personal (and often marginal) testimony inspires and draws forth the testimonies of others.[13] In this situation, according to Anna Carter Florence, the preacher seals her words to the scriptural witness in spite of and, if necessary, beyond the blessing of the community of faith, and testifies on behalf of one's self and those who are similarly in the margins of the community and its traditions.[14] Within counter-testimonial homiletics, memory is considered a site of contestation. Preaching testifies *on behalf of* the (often lost) memories of self and similar others, and *in spite of* the de-legitimation of one's memory by those within the church courts historically and in the present situation.

A third model is *ethnographic homiletics*. Leonora Tubbs Tisdale has developed an approach to the homiletical task closely wedded to demographics, ethnography, and congregational study.[15] She shows how preachers can engage in guided interviews; study archival materials such as church bulletins, old sermons, fundraising brochures, and newsletters; do demographic analysis; consider architecture and visual arts; study rituals, special events, and activities; and observe people and their usual practices—all in favor of theologically exegeting congregations in a way that resembles exegeting a written text. At the end of this process, Tisdale invites

---

13. Rose, *Sharing the Word*.
14. Florence, *Preaching as Testimony*.
15. Tisdale, *Preaching as Local Theology and Folk Art*.

Preaching and the Personal

preachers to make strategic, practical theological decisions. These decisions can take five different shapes:

1. Preaching can affirm and confirm the right imaginings of the congregational heart.
2. Preaching can stretch the limits of the congregational imagination.
3. Preaching can invert the assumed ordering of the imaginal world of the congregation.
4. Preaching can challenge and judge the false imaginings of the congregational heart.
5. Preaching can help congregations imagine worlds they have not yet seen (or even imagined).[16]

For Tisdale, congregational "imagination" should be studied, and then constructively engaged. A key element in this engagement is the business of shaping the community's memory. In this model, memory, in all of its aspects, is deeply embedded within the signs and symbols used by the community. These signs and symbols are ethnographically uncovered, analyzed, and then (re)negotiated from the pulpit. Listeners and their memories are studied in order to increase the effectiveness of the preacher's work of memory-construction and enhancement.

The fourth model might be called *biblical constructionist homiletics*. This approach incorporates a fundamental theological suspicion of the value of reception in the homiletical process. Grounded in post-liberal thought and virtue ethics, purveyors of this model argue that the goal of preaching is to use the biblical narrative to render or construct a unique Christian identity that will radically re-shape or re-script any prior identity. The early work of Charles Campbell[17] and the ongoing work of William Willimon[18] provide strong support for what must be considered a fundamentally anti-receptionist and social constructionist homiletic.

16. Ibid., 111–20.
17. Campbell, *Preaching Jesus*.
18. See especially Willimon and Hauerwas, *Preaching to Strangers*; Willimon, *The Intrusive Word*; Willimon, *Preaching to the Unbaptized*.

In this model, all forms of memory that draw resources from outside the biblical narrative are suspect. Memory is a site of unidirectional (Bible-to-listener) reconstruction. Memory is invariably misled by one's experiences, and requires rescripting by the biblical text and the Jesus who is rendered therein. Preaching is catechetical and improvisational, teaching the biblical narrative in a way that will re-construct memory and identity and encourage new performances of the memory script provided by the biblical text itself.

COLLABORATIVE PREACHING

Although all of the approaches mentioned above have much to commend them, they all contain one limitation. With the possible exception of counter-testimonial homiletics, they operate primarily at the level at which memory is *represented* (or signified) within congregations and culture. They do not address the ways in which memory is, in fact, *performed* minute by minute in the interhuman and interactive life of a given community, and the role that preaching might play in the immediate reflexive nurturance of that performance. In order to accomplish this, preaching must be embedded within a living dialogical and ritual-performative process in which memory-in-community is created, shaped, and put on display. Communication theorists call this an accent on the "post-semiotic" or "post-representational" aspects of communication.[19] The preacher focuses on the ways in which memory is being performed and shaped within dialogue between very different persons, embodying diverse forms of memory. Of course, this dialogue relies heavily upon the larger semiotic field of theological ideas and constructs within a culture, a tradition, and a congregation. This way of thinking is post-semiotic, not a-semiotic. The accent is placed more upon the *event* or *eventfulness* of theological communication, its "in-the-nowness" and the unique ways in which memory is articulated and embodied in this very particular moment and place, and less upon controlling and manipulating larger structures and systems of signs.

19. Stewart, *Language as Articulate Contact*.

Preaching and the Personal

In order to place preaching into the middle of this process of "in-the-now" memory work in relation to the Bible, I have encouraged a method of preaching called "collaborative preaching" in which preachers are encouraged to hold sermon "roundtables" before preaching. In these roundtables lay persons, from the center of church life to its margins (and beyond), are involved in a process of sermon brainstorming each week. These roundtables change membership regularly, so that an "in group" cannot develop. I also encourage preachers to leave behind clergy lectionary study groups where a standard form of biblical interpretation is encouraged and the theology that is produced is primarily clerical in nature and to interpret biblical texts with ordinary people in a variety of social locations. This usually means leaving the pastor's study altogether for the process of brainstorming sermons and perhaps even leaving the church building, preparing the sermon in a public place. Sermon roundtables meet in a variety of places, including public buildings, homes, and shelters. The goal is to come to terms with the unique, strange, and sometimes bizarre interpretations of the gospel that are around us in our culture, in the minds and hearts of good church people, and latent within the recesses of our own lives.

No matter how such a model of preaching is construed, the preacher is re-imagined as the host of a conversation about ancient texts (and thus a memory-work conversation), rather than as a prophet, herald (*keryg*), witness, or storyteller. In essence, the preacher is seen as someone who is initiating, facilitating, and stewarding an ongoing conversation in and through which the congregation is engaging its past and talking itself into becoming more deeply and fully Christian in the present. This process accentuates, highlights, and even dramatizes the many ways in which a congregation is uttering (creating) or constituting in this very moment its own biblical-theological memory. While the sermon remains a single-party communication event, it is embedded within and re-presents an actual interactive, multiparty communication process in which a group of ordinary people are discerning, articulating, and practicing memory.

PROXIMATE BODIES PERFORMING MEMORY

According to sociologist Pierre Bourdieu, the body is central to the *habitus* or "feel for the game" within a community of discourse. This is because the body is the place of memory, preservation, and practice of one's *habitus*.[20] Collaborative preaching attends carefully to the body, or more properly, to bodies in proximity and interaction, and to the ways these bodies contribute to the structuring of memory and practices of theological interpretation and imagination. Of particular significance here are the ways those gathered to the sacred text *remember* the foundational events portrayed therein. This is not a static process, and involves the embodiment, preservation, and practice of several basic forms of memory. Collaborative preachers learn to: (1) identify ways that memory is performed; (2) nurture these performances in roundtable groups and in other arenas of community life; and (3) re-perform these performances for the larger community in sermons and liturgies. After nearly twenty years of collaborative preaching and listening to other collaborative preachers, it is possible to identify six ways that memory is typically performed in collaborative preaching groups.

In the first instance, memory is embodied in a way that might be labeled *kerygmatic* in nature. Here, memory is largely practiced through the sharing of oral traditions and the passing on of "family stories." Like the *kerygmatic* narratives in the book of Acts, repeated over and over again by Jesus's followers, members of the sermon roundtable gravitate to familiar, time-worn features of the text, accenting well-known, timeless elements or "Sunday-School interpretations" that seem to have always been significant for the community of faith over time. These interpretations are "hegemonic" in that they "go without saying." The text is treated in a primarily devotional fashion. Members of the group look for simple maxims that seem obvious in the English translation. The cyclical, repetitive nature of the liturgical year and lectionary preaching often supports this form of memory in the church as familiar texts and themes are repeated and recycled. Participants experience certain texts as paradigmatic for faith, and certain turns of phrase, patterns of

---

20. Bourdieu, *Outline of a Theory of Practice*, 94.

thought, and expressive forms take on qualities of ritual. Memory is embodied as a form of *desire* or longing for a remembered and anticipated emotional *home*. Memories generate shared feelings that take us into familiar sacred spaces and rituals of meaning, orienting us within the community in commonly understood ways.

The second form of memory bodied forth in sermon roundtables is *mimetic* or imitative in nature. In this model, the past is remembered as an *original to be copied*. Interpreters typically point to moments in the text-in-translation, identifying analogies in their own lives. Often they will tell stories from their own experience that seem, in their own minds, to be more or less equivalent to something discovered in the text. The goal of mimetic memory is to imitate the past in similar words, postures, patterns of thinking, and emotions. If Mary sat at the feet of Jesus, we too should embody a similar posture in our own lives. If the disciples "took up their nets and followed" Jesus, we should do likewise. Mimetic forms of memory express a deep desire for the Christian community to become a body of believers who are *like* some model from the past.

The third form of memory is *reconstructive*. This form of memory is historical in nature and very concerned with accuracy. Members of the roundtable who desire to represent and preserve this kind of memory show up at meetings with commentaries or sheets of paper printed from Internet websites tucked under their arms. They often indicate in various ways the importance of doing some careful "research." If they have already done such research, they look for openings to share this special knowledge with the group. If they haven't, they will ask the presiding minister/preacher any number of (difficult) questions about the history behind the text, its author, community of origin, and so on. They are concerned to hear from historians and biblical theologians, and to discover ideas or vicissitudes that may exist behind the text, in its historical context. They are less concerned to re-member the past by imitating it. Instead, they want the preacher to reconstruct the ancient world so that the community can live in *accurate continuity* with a community from the past. The goal is to measure and synchronize the community's remembering so that it faithfully reconstructs the past in today's world.

A fourth type of memory is *performative*. This kind of biblical interpreter comes to the sermon roundtable concerned with the way the text "feels" or "sounds." They say such things as: "this sounds like . . . (a used car salesman, a song, a teacher, a poet, a troubled person, a complaint, etc.)," "this story makes me . . . ," "these words are words of invitation that . . . ," "this is a hard word to hear, isn't it," or "it is as if this whole parable conspires to . . ." This person brings into the roundtable a keen interest in how the language of the text works on us. Commonsense meanings within the text and historical continuities are pushed into the background, and the performative aspects of the language of the text (in translation) become most important.

For these persons, memory is not a form of desire, mimesis, or reconstruction, but a *re-performance*. Similar to ritual practices such as celebrating the Lord's Supper or Passover, memory involves us in a re-performance of the religious past in a way that makes it functionally present. Expressive, mimetic and historical elements are subsumed by dramatic, ritualistic, and performative attempts to capture the way that a past event would have sounded, felt, and had an impact on its original audience. Memory is bound up with particular forms of speech and how they work to shape consciousness and action.

A fifth type of memory is *thematic*. These interpreters usually want to focus memory thematically. They are often consumed with certain ideological (theological, psychological, spiritual, etc.) themes that are meaningful to them and that they associate with the memory and ongoing commitments of the church. No matter what the text, it must be about "a personal relationship with Jesus Christ," or "liberation," or "Celtic spirituality," and so on. Typically, in the sermon roundtable, this person will gravitate toward a pivotal moment in the biblical witness that focuses these thematic claims. These claims are usually framed as potentially transformative in nature—a pivotal moment in the text engendering pivotal claims on one's life. In this process, memory takes on a thematic and evocative shape. The past is entirely framed within a set of ideas, beliefs, and assumptions that are meant to evoke similar insight in others.

The sixth type of memory, found increasingly in roundtable groups today, is *counter-memory*. Counter-memory arises out of the suspicion of all traditions. Members of sermon roundtables attempt to attend to *others* within the margins of the biblical text, and in the margins of the Christian tradition, whose voices may not have had a place at the table as the tradition was defined. This interpreter usually comes to the group "down under" some contextual issue or concern. They use issues, questions, events, hunches, suspicions, insights, or crises arising from contemporary experience as catalysts for the discovery of hidden or latent trajectories of meaning within the ancient text. Tough questions and issues spark new insights into the meaning of the text that were not seen before. The interpreter, struggling for meaning, is often forced to move to a deep theological or historical dimension of the text in order to find a trajectory that correlates with the cultural or experiential issue at hand. This means going "beneath" the text, using a conceptual hermeneutic that appeals to a deep biblical principle rumbling beneath the particular text at hand. Counter-memory has a heuristic quality. Memory is bent toward finding trajectories of meaning from the past that are hidden from view, awaiting this particular moment in history and this particular situation to be drawn out into plain view. This hidden trajectory might not be unique. It could have been discovered before, but it is always developing further implications and meanings as it is interpreted in different epochs and situations. For instance, during the Penn State sexual abuse scandal in November, 2011, a sermon roundtable member found herself struggling toward deeper trajectories of meaning regarding forgiveness as the group considered the command by Jesus to forgive "seventy-seven times" (Matt 18: 21–22, NIV). In the end, she asserted that "forgiveness without justice is empty."

PREACHING AND BIBLICAL STUDY AS MUTUALLY REINFORCING PERFORMANCES OF MEMORY

In the vacuum of performed memory in the postmodern situation, collaborative preaching becomes a significant opportunity for a community to both *perform memory* (in a Bible study), and then to witness *memory in performance* (in the sermon and liturgy). According to Baz Kershaw, this kind of practice "doubles" memory, and "creates a highly complex disjunction of ontologies: in effect a limit case that paradoxically asserts both the difference between and identity of past and present . . ."[21] In sermon roundtables, participants experience the difference between their experiences and the past, and the variety of ways in which memory struggles to unite the two. In the ritual practice of worship and preaching, they give themselves over to the identity of past and present, re-visiting the original scene of representation itself, in the present moment. As practical theologians of memory, therefore, collaborative preachers create spaces in which memory can be performed, engage deeply and generously in the community's performance, and then share aspects of that performance for all to witness in liturgy and preaching. In this way, parallel and connected practices of performing memory become central to the life of the community of faith.

It is possible to note how practicing memory in collaborative preaching groups mirrors, in many ways, current hermeneutical models. Kerygmatic and mimetic practices correspond to hermeneutical models that emphasize the discovery of dynamic analogies or equivalencies between words and propositions within texts and contemporary experience. Reconstructive practices of memory correspond roughly to historical critical methods of exegesis and interpretation. Performative memory corresponds with scholarly interest in literary and rhetorical tropes, and in reader-response. Thematic memory has many parallels to forms of theological hermeneutics. Counter-memory runs parallel to some types of contextual and sociological interpretation. It may be possible, therefore, to develop important relationships between practices of

21. Kershaw, *The Radical in Performance*, 166–67.

memory in the church and theories of biblical interpretation. At the same time, it might be possible to re-imagine biblical hermeneutics as part of the "practical theology of memory." At the very least, one might suggest the need to build reflection on the practical theology of memory into the ways in which we think about practices of interpreting scripture. Instead of seeing approaches to biblical hermeneutics as mutually exclusive or as isolated sub-disciplines they might be seen as performances of different forms of memory, and as contributing to the enrichment of these forms of memory in congregations and communities of faith.

CONCLUSION

If memory is to be kept from degenerating into a theatrical prop on a stage devoid of any real nurturing of actual performances of memory, it may be crucial for preachers to make use of post-semiotic, dialogical models of biblical interpretation and preaching designed to invigorate the many ways that biblical interpretation and memory are caught up together and negotiated *in the here and now*. Such approaches challenge preachers to become practical theologians of memory, ready to enter fully into collaborative preaching as able nurturers of the double performance of memory in the community of faith today.

6

"It Ain't Necessarily So"
Resistance Preaching and Womanist Thought[1]

VALERIE BRIDGEMAN

IN 1935, THE MUSICAL "Porgy and Bess" made headlines because it was the first all African American cast to take to Broadway stages. Written by George and Ira Gershwin, it pushed American publics to see African American life. It was, to be sure, stereotypical in a lot of ways. When "Sportin' Life," a drug dealer, questions devotion of churchgoing listeners, he sings, "De things dat yo' liable to read in de Bible, it ain't necessarily so." His words are heretical and scandalous. What he does in the song, and what people in marginalized communities continue to do, is to suggest that not every thing we read in the Bible may be taken at its face value. We must question

---

1. A portion of this address is modified from my PhD dissertation, "Like a Woman in Labor: Toward a Womanist Reading of the Book of Micah," Baylor University, 2002, and from a lecture I did for the Gardner C. Taylor Lecture Series at Duke Divinity School, October 7, 2008.

texts in order to interpret them. "Sportin' Life" especially poked at biblical literalism. In some ways, Womanist scholars continue poking in the same place.

DEFINING WOMANIST IN THE BIBLICAL AND THEOLOGICAL WORLDS OF SCHOLARSHIP

African American women literary critics embraced the term "Womanist" from the first time it appeared in the writings of Alice Walker in 1983. These critics developed methodologies for reading and interpreting writings, especially works by North American writers, and most especially the works of women of color. African American women Christian theologians and ethicists also found the term compelling and a crop of writings by these scholars using what they called Womanist strategies began to appear. The chief goal and appropriation of the term, according to these scholars, is to prioritize issues facing African American women, and by extension women of color everywhere. Emilie Townes, a Womanist ethicist, defines Womanists in the following way:

> Perhaps the most common understanding of Womanist is that she is a woman committed to an integrated analysis of race, gender, and class. This [analysis] arises from a deep concern to address the shortcomings of traditional feminist and Black theological modes of discourse. The former has a long legacy of ignoring race and class issues. The latter has disregarded gender and class. Both modes of discourse have begun to address these internal flaws. Yet Womanist reflection maintains its critical perspective of feminist and African American traditional ways of analytical reflection.
>   This critical perspective extends to Eurocentric discourse as well. Much of what Womanist thought seeks to debunk is the notion of universals and absolutes. Womanist thought is intentionally and unapologetically biased . . . for a diverse and faithful community of witnesses.

These witnesses are an active force for love and justice in the midst of oppression and fallenness.[2]

Some African American women scholars have sought to differentiate Womanist scholarship from its mother (if only a step-parent), feminist scholarship and its father (step-parent), Black Theology. While there are inevitable similarities, Womanist scholars would echo the sentiment of the late radical activist poet, Audre Lorde that "Black feminism is not white feminism in blackface."[3] Nor is it Black theology in drag.

Here, it is worth extensively quoting Emilie M. Townes's essay, "Searching for Paradise in a World of Theme Parks." She says:

> ". . .taking its cues from black theology and feminist theology, Womanist theology cannot and must not merely accept methodologies or constructs of theological reflection that do not consider with ongoing rigor the experience of African American women and the diversities found within black womanhood and the larger African American community. In both an intercommunal dialogue with other racial and ethnic groups and an intra-communal conversation among black folk, Womanist thought seeks to explore the nature of oppression as it has a peculiar impact on the lives of black women. This is done with an eye toward the nature of how this may or may not manifest itself in the lives of men, children, the aged, differing sexualities, persons of various class locations, and so forth . . . Race is joined with a host of other

---

2. Townes, "Introduction," 1–2. For a sampling of the ways in which African American women scholars are wrestling with definition, see also Townes, "A Black Feminist Critique of Feminist Theology," 189–91; Brown, "God Is As Christ Does," 7–16; Cannon, "The Emergence of Black Feminist Consciousness"; Durrah, "Triple Jeopardy," 44–53; Grant, *White Women's Christ and Black Women's Jesus*; and Williams, "The Color of Feminism," 2–58. In addition, see all the essays in the section on Womanist Theology, 255–351, in James H. Cone and Gayraud S. Wilmore, *Black Theology*, vol. 2.

3. Lorde, "Sexism," 60. Lorde never adopted the term "Womanist" in her writings because she was concerned that a separate African American women's movement would dilute the strength of all women fighting patriarchal oppression. She preferred to challenge the feminist movement about its own racism.

materialities of black life in a hermeneutic of liberation and transformation."[4]

CONFRONTATIONAL HERMENEUTICS

The necessary question, then, leads to how reading/believing communities determine what texts within the canon are to be regarded "Scripture"—authoritative, informative, and transformative. Ideological criticisms (Feminists, Womanists, Black Liberations, Queer, e.g.) allow for a resistance to the canon with a "canon within the canon" to critique, wrestle with, and reject—when necessary—texts that continue to support and promote oppression of any peoples. One need only remember the now canonical story of Howard Thurman's grandmother who declared that she would never read Paul again because the apostle promoted slavery. Or as Cannon says, the thoughtful interpreter must ask the ethicist's question of moral concerns: "That is, 'it is truly here, but is it right?'"[5]

Cannon's words led me to embrace Kirk-Duggan's term, confrontational hermeneutic. Kirk-Duggan rightly says that a Womanist must question, be suspicious of, turn on its head, and use any other means that will expose oppression as well as liberation within the text. It is just as important to know the destructive tendencies of the text as it is to know the salvific ones. Or as biblical scholar Renita Weems has noted, communities give legitimacy and potency to individual interpretations.[6] It is true that what you are *capable* of seeing and asking of texts depends on where you stand. Womanists read knowing that meaning and relevance in these texts must be wrestled from prevailing scholarship and from male narrators and male audiences of texts.[7] Meaning occurs in confrontation with biblical texts and real lives. And when embracing the text requires loving a God that does not love you, then the text must, as a faithful

4. Townes, "In a World of Theme Parks," 111.

5. Cannon, "The Emergence of Black Feminist Consciousness," 33.

6. Weems, "Reading *Her* Way through the Struggle," 62. See also, Fish, *Is There a Text in This Class?*; and Penchansky, "Up for Grabs," 35–41.

7. Weems, "Do You See What I See?," 31.

witness, be resisted. Preaching must say "no" to a word that deals death. That is the Womanist way. Meaning and proclamation happens on the meeting ground between congregation and the need, not only to survive, but also to thrive. Sometimes, the preacher must faithfully say, "It ain't (necessarily) so."

A TURN TOWARD PREACHING

How, then, do we apply a homiletic to Womanist thought? Following Womanist thought, Womanist preaching is radically open as evidenced in the questions it asks and the emotions it exposes. As Weems notes, "The preaching task begins with getting in touch with the emotion of the text—not so much *what* it says but how it says what it says. Seminary gave me the tools I needed to ask the questions I had, questions that allowed me to read against the grain of the text, questions admittedly the biblical text never meant to answer."[8]

For example, starting with the statement made by Alice Walker's character, Celie, in *The Color Purple*, we wonder out loud how reading this text will liberate, uplift, and encourage poor, black women. When Celie insists that God sounds like every white man she ever knew, she is chastened by Miss Shug to "hush," lest God hears her complaint. Celie says, "Let 'im hear me, I say. If he ever listened to poor colored women the world would be a different place, I can tell you."[9]

Womanist preaching believes that God is, in fact, listening to "poor colored women." Dr. Johnnetta Cole, speaking as then-president of Spelman College during convocation, asserted this notion in an address titled, "Jesus is a Sister." She maintained that an African American sister "knows oppression because of the race problem, the woman question, and the poverty predicament," and that Jesus sided with such people, so identifying with them that he could be called one. But Cole understood that Womanist proclamation goes much further than naming and making clear oppression;

---

8. Weems, "How Will Our Preaching Be Remembered?," 26–29.
9. Walker, *The Color Purple*, 187.

such preaching also affirms that we are to understand that Jesus also works with such women in resistance and victory, not merely in oppression and struggle.[10] Such a homiletic qualifies as what Womanist-pastor-preacher the Reverend Dr. Elaine Flake at New York City's Greater Allen Temple AME Church calls "a hermeneutic of healing," whereby we are responsible to confront a violent culture with a healing one, and to dismantle anti-female attitudes, "even those perpetuated in Scripture"[11]—in other words, to resist. Donna Allen, examining the preaching of Prathia Hall Wynn, discovered this principle in play in Hall's preaching.

Resistance for preaching means always keeping before oneself one's own particularity and social location. It means paying attention to how texts act on the preacher, first. It means noticing the ethical implications of an interpretation that consciously asks questions of the underbelly of texts, questions about the triple jeopardy of racism, classism, and sexism. It means asking whether God is listening to poor, colored women.

Another strategy for me is to embrace a confrontational hermeneutic that allows for "righteous indignation" at the "the subtlety of oppression, the ways that biblical women's roles and women-oriented metaphors have often been used to punish, demean and control women."[12] Kirk-Duggan rightly says that a Womanist must question, be suspicious of, turn on its head, and use any other means that will expose oppression as well as liberation within the text. It is just as important to know the destructive tendencies of the text, as it is to know the salvific ones. It's a matter of survival (and thriving), and people outside acceptable definitions of "normative" know that "survival is not an academic skill."[13]

As Renita Weems has noted, communities give legitimacy and potency to individual interpretations.[14] Since all readings

10. Cole, "Jesus is a Sister," 152.
11. Flake, *God in Her Midst*, 4.
12. Kirk-Duggan, "What Difference Does Difference Make," 268.
13. Lorde, "The Master's Tools," 112.
14. Weems, "Reading *Her* Way through the Struggle," 62. See also, Fish, *Is There a Text in This Class? Authority of Interpretative Communities*; Penchansky, "Up for Grabs," 35–41.

are "interested,"[15] some times competing interests vie for readers' loyalties. Sometimes, texts themselves reject concerns of reading communities. In a given setting, it may be impossible to entertain competing understandings of the text, as those interpretations may be diametrically opposed to one another. For instance, ways in which most Christian homosexuals and many evangelicals read Leviticus 18 and 20 are irreconcilable.[16] It is true that what you are *capable* of seeing and asking of texts depends on where you stand. We read knowing that meaning and relevance in these texts must be wrestled from prevailing scholarship and from the male narrators and male audiences of texts.[17] Weems maintains that meaning, in a revelatory sense, takes place "when the values and interests of the narrators coincide with those of the readers."[18] Meaning, then, is not inherent to texts or readers, but is discovered somewhere on the meeting grounds between them. Or as Margaret B. Adams so aptly notes, "We come, as always, with all of our ideological habits; and God meets us, our ideologies, and the text, all jumbled up together. The sense that we make of this crowded meeting is what we call 'interpreting scripture'; our ongoing work of telling the story rightly."[19] Our task, as Townes has charged us, is "to be very particular about the particular—and explore the vastness of it . . . we are trying to understand the assortments of African American life."[20]

When I teach students, whether in class or in workshops throughout the country, I am mindful of this "jumbled" meeting space. I am mindful that it creates tension, and therefore the possibility of resistance. I often invite students to "meet the resistance" in texts and in the room among listeners. I want would-be Womanist preachers to look for the places of departure from "normative" interpretations and proclamations in texts, especially when the

---

15. Clines, *Interested Parties*.

16. See Penchansky, "Up for Grabs," on allowing competing interpretations to exist. For a discussion on the problem of reading others' lives for them, see Alcoff, "The Problem of Speaking for Others," 5–32.

17. Weems, "Do You See What I See?," 31.

18. Ibid., 32.

19. Adam, "This is *My* Story, This is *My* Song," 223.

20. Townes, "Searching for Paradise," 112.

norm calls for people to submit to domineering, patriarchal, death-dealing decisions. I include the notion of the "survival principle" as a part of the interlocking analysis that must be done in order to find Good News to preach. This call is not one of being a contrarian for contrary's sake. Rather, Womanist preachers must know going in that biblical texts are fraught with danger. And the work before us is salvation, not just of the personal kind, but also of the social kind. Our task is to proclaim a vision from a liberating and delighting God that provides abundant life for all who hear.

CONCLUSION

In the end, to read, translate, interpret, and proclaim as a Womanist is hard work because it calls for openness to the voices of Africana women, a charge to make those voices clear and prophetic in a cacophony of voices, and to hold accountable the church, our understanding of the Divine, and such women themselves to full and complete health, wholeness, and liberation. By making the margins visible, we make the center whole. When resisting texts that do not bring life, even preaching against such texts, Womanist preaching requires an unswerving stare into texts that teach and speak death, risk the well-being of people, and choosing to resist or to reject them. We remind the believing community that we stand in the tradition of prophets, continuous from the ancient Hebrew texts we claim as Christian texts into these witness-bound words of disciples. We bear witness to a God peeking from these pages but not bound by or to them.

When it's all said and done, I find I do not want to, nor intend, to abandon the biblical texts, even if I judge certain texts less significant and even dangerous to me in some private moment of brutal honesty. I both celebrate and resist at the well of these words. I am recklessly, hopelessly, and willingly entangled in the web of surviving with and without them. I leave you with a poem I wrote that makes more poignantly, I hope, this point:

The Holy Book[21]

It's in me,
the story and the telling.
I keep wanting to get the story out
but I feel trapped sometimes
by my own loyalties,
afraid to discover a God
different from my heritage,
different from the texts.

Sometimes,
my experience rails against,
lashes out against scriptures that speak death.
Other times, the spirit of life
leaps from the pages,
enslaving and empowering,
giving me a *go on, girl*
in my legs and my heart.

Sometimes,
the text is sedative,
providing a peace that lets me sleep
and allows tomorrow to arrive
unannounced by worry.

The Grand Book is sacred, yes,
but not because its jots and tittles are aligned.
Rather, because the Book talks,
it breathes, it begs conversation,
and unlike humans,
it is not afraid
of disagreements.

At times,
I thought God would strike me dead
for such rebellions.
Imagine my delight when
I found myself—still standing,
and God smiling at my holy defiance,
my refusal to *just believe.*

---

21. Bridgeman Davis, "Response in Prose and Poetry," 215–16.

7

Liberating Preaching
Hispanic Hermeneutics and Homiletics: Collaborative and Contextual Approaches to Preaching

DAVID CORTÉS-FUENTES

HISPANIC AMERICAN HOMILETICS: A RECENT UNDERTAKING

HISPANIC HOMILETICS HAS EVOLVED from a traditional art imitating Anglo-Saxon styles and themes to a more autochthonous, critical, and liberating movement in recent years. As a field of study and research, it is fairly recent, especially within the Hispanic protestant tradition. It begins with the arrival of the earliest protestant missionaries to Latin America who brought with them their homiletic manuals and preaching traditions from North America.

Pablo A. Jiménez[1] identifies three stages in the development of a Hispanic homiletics theory: transculturation, inculturation, and contextualization.

Transculturation is characterized by the missionary movement of North America into Latin America. Most of the early missionaries tended to be more conservative and had an "anti-Catholic" attitude. These missionaries provided and translated manuals for lay preachers and ministers such as the books of C. H. Spurgeon, John A Broadus, Andrew W. Blackwood, and J. D. Crane. Theirs was a deductive, neo-classical understanding of sermon design, an Anglo-American worldview, a "free-church" perspective approach to homiletics that discouraged the use of lectionaries and did little to relate the sermon to the liturgy. It appealed particularly to well-educated candidates for ministry.

The second stage, Inculturation, is related to a group of learned Hispanic ministers who became the first Latin American scholars in the field of homiletics. These are preachers and professors such as Angel Mergal (Evangelical Seminary of Puerto Rico), Orlando E. Costas (Latin American Bible Institute, Costa Rica), Osvaldo Motessi (Northern Baptist Theological Seminary), and Cecilio Arrastía (McCormick Theological Seminary in Chicago, and the Evangelical Seminary of Puerto Rico), whose publications in journals and religious magazines established the model for the ideal preaching for most protestant pastors in Latin America and Hispanics preachers in the United States. Some of the most important contributions of these homileticians were their emphasis on the aesthetic quality of the discipline, a communal understanding of preaching, a commitment to the local church, a ministry of identity and solidarity, and their emphasis on the use of resources from Spanish literature for preaching.

The third stage of the development of Hispanic homiletics theory, Contextualization, is exemplified by the developments of a distinctive theological movement of the last three decades. The birth and growth of a Hispanic American theology is distinguished by a theological reflection that is contextual and intentionally

---

1. González and Jiménez, *Púlpito,* 3–16.

expresses the experiences of the Latino communities in the United States. The point of departure for a theological reflection from Hispanic / Latino and Latina perspective is the social location and the daily reality that the Latino community experiences in the United States. This is characterized by the particular religious experiences of the Hispanic community, and the marginalization suffered by the Latino people.

According to Jiménez (and many other Latino and Latina theologians), Hispanic theology advances a methodology that advocates a *praxis of liberation* that seeks the transformation of the oppressive reality endured by the Latino people. Scholars such as Orlando E. Costas, Justo L. González, Pablo A. Jiménez, Samuel Pagán, and Daniel Rodríguez-Díaz are called pioneer scholars whose contributions to the field of Hispanic homiletics is shaping the present and future generations of Hispanic preachers both in the United States and Latin America. One of the characteristics shared by these Hispanic homiletics scholars is the understanding of homiletics as a task that is closely related to Hispanic culture and is informed by the experience of Latinos. The books and anthologies edited by these scholars established a pattern of theological reflection done in collaboration and mutual feedback by the different writers and preachers. This is a characteristic of Hispanic American theological ethos that is called *Teología en conjunto* (collegial or collaborative theology).[2] A classic example of "teología en conjunto" is what Justo L. González calls "Fuenteovejuna Theology." The name "Fuenteovejuna" refers to the name of a small town whose people rebelled and killed their tyrannical ruler and commander (Commander don Fernán Gómez). When a judge-inquisitor tried to find the guilty party, the whole town answered the same way to the inquisitor's question: *"¿Quién mató al comendador?"* (Who killed the commander?) Their answer was, *"Fuenteovejuna, señor"* (Fuenteovejuna, my lord). To the inquiry of who "Fuenteovejuna" was, the unanimous response was, *"Fuenteovejuna, todos a una"* (Fuenteovejuna, all are one). The unanimous answer reflects the idea that

---

2. Rodríguez and Martell-Otero, eds., *Teología en conjunto*.

the whole town united in solidarity is the real responsible party for the death of the commander and not any individual in particular.[3]

A common feature of these homileticians is a deep appreciation for the serious and informed study of the scriptures. Justo L. González's *Mañana: Christian Theology from a Hispanic Perspective* includes a chapter dedicated to an insightful description of Hispanic biblical hermeneutics that he called, "Reading the Bible in Spanish."[4] González expanded his ideas in *Santa Biblia: Reading the Bible Through Hispanic Eyes*, where he describes the characteristics of North American Hispanic/Latino hermeneutics through topics of gender discrimination, poverty, Mestizaje, exile, and solidarity. They share a reading of the Biblical text informed by a hermeneutics of suspicion, "a methodological principle that assumes that any interpretation of the text, especially those from traditional Euro-American interpreters, conceal the ideological and political interests of the interpreters." Latino interpreters believe that there is no impartial interpretation that is free from the interpreter's interests. Hispanic/Latino theologians are especially suspicious of interpretations that ignore the social location of the text, the interpreter, and the community. So, in their reading and interpretation of the Scriptures, Hispanic homiletics affirms that the experience of Latinos and Latinas in their practice of faith is a source for theological reflection and theological understanding. It also pays special attention to many themes including issues of justice, race, gender, class, and immigration. The works of Ada María Isasi-Díaz are classic examples of Hispanic/Latino understanding of the importance of faith practice as a theological reflection.[5] According to Isasi-Díaz, the reading of the Bible must be done to help the oppressed in their struggle for liberation. The Bible as a whole is an example of the lived experiences of God's people. God's revelation happens in the midst of these lives. This revelation, according to Isasi-Díaz, is

---

3. González, *Mañana*, 28–30.
4. Ibid., 75–87.
5. Isasi-Díaz, "The Bible and Mujerista Theology," 261–69; and Isasi-Díaz, "La Palabra de Dios en nosotras," 86–100.

Preaching and the Personal

where God's people come to understand who God is and what are God's demands for humans.⁶

HISPANIC HERMENEUTICS: A SURVEY

The major proponents of Hispanic American hermeneutics are men and women representing a number of different Christian traditions. Many are first-generation Hispanic Americans that moved to the United States for a variety of reasons. Although there are specific emphases in their many contributions to Hispanic-American theology, some fundamental characteristics and topics are shared by them all. Scholars such as Virgilio Elizondo (The Mexican American Experience), Orlando Costas (Galilee as periphery), Justo L. González (Mañana theology), Harold Recinos (El Barrio [Ghetto] theology), Ada María Isasi-Díaz (Mujerista theology), Fernando F. Segovia (Diaspora hermeneutics) and Francisco García-Treto (East of Eden theology) bring to the table a theological refection that emphasizes the importance of the experience of the Latino community as the hermeneutical lenses through which Hispanics read and interpret the Scriptures. Issues such as the experience of marginality, gender discrimination, poverty, Mestizaje, exile, and solidarity permeate both the theological reflection and hermeneutics of these Latino theologians.

Justo L. González calls Latino preachers to recognize that the doctrine of incarnation implies that theology, in order to be truly Christian, must be incarnated.⁷ This implies that "it must take flesh in each culture and situation, in each time and circumstance." He also calls the Latino and Latina preachers to affirm a "theology that is ours" (without ceasing to be universal), affirmative (the affirmation of God's love for us), in solidarity (the church as the body of Christ), and with a sense of eschatological subversion (it is a theology of hope of a future of justice, peace, equality, and solidarity). Latino hermeneutics read Scripture not just to interpret it (and to control its meaning) but to be interpreted by the text and moved

---

6. Isasi-Díaz, *La Lucha Continues*, 220.
7. González and Jiménez, *Púlpito*, 17–38.

into concrete action for transformation. This reading of Scripture is done in awareness of the culture and language (the paradigm of *mestizo*).

The social, economic, and political issues that affect Hispanic Americans also play an important role in the interpretation of Scripture, especially when most of Latinos live as underprivileged. Informed by Latin American Liberation Theology, Latinos identify themselves with the poor and affirm God's special interest and "preferential option" for the poor. By "preferential option" for the poor, Latino theologians refer to the biblical witness of God special care for the most vulnerable in society, especially the powerless people that may become victims of exploitation and abuse. For instance, the Exodus story shows God's preferential option for the poor when God takes the cause of the Hebrew slaves and liberated them from the oppression. This option for the poor informs Latino homiletics by calling the church to actions of solidarity, empowerment, and social transformation. Preaching becomes not an end into itself but a means by which the good news of the Kingdom become tools for justice, liberty, and affirmation of their Hispanic heritage.

A special concern for Hispanic theologians and church members is the issue of immigration. Although most Latinos are born citizens of the United States, many members of the congregations are recent immigrants, some of them without documentation. But the major issue is the general assumption by the dominant culture that Hispanics are immigrants, even when most of them did not cross the border, but the border crossed them. Finally, the issue of identity informs Hispanic hermeneutic because by being bilingual and bicultural, in continuous contact with the land of their ancestors and relatives; they are continually reminded by the dominant culture and their families that they are different. Thus, social and ethnic identity is a continuous issue for Hispanics. In one of his most recent books, Pablo A. Jiménez discusses an approach to homiletics that takes in consideration the new technological advances, the context of the audience, and the challenges raised by culture, social justice, liberation, and postmodernity.[8]

---

8 Jiménez, *La Predicación en el siglo XXI*.

GENERAL CHARACTERISTICS AND FUTURE

Some consistent features characterize Hispanic hermeneutics and impact Hispanic homiletics. Foremost is the conviction that the Bible is a liberating text. Pastors and preachers read in the Bible the life and the struggles of the Hispanic community, anticipated or told paradigmatically in the Bible story (Segovia). The cultural and social symbol of Mestizaje and the experience of marginalization or living at the periphery is a second characteristic feature. This social location and experience allows the Hispanic communities to identify themselves with both the exodus and exile biblical stories. Living at the margin becomes a locus for theological reflection and the understanding of God's revelation.

The experience of marginality serves as a springboard for a reading of resistance that produces a critical stance calling into question the present social order in the light of an ideology of a liberating Kingdom of God. Hispanics also finds a correlation between the experience of the characters in the biblical story and their own experience. But this identification is not just at a superficial level, but an analogy of relationships, power structures, and hopes of the people (F. F. Segovia). Finally, Hispanic reading offers a vision of eschatological hope. Through this eschatology of hope, Latinos interpret present experiences of poverty, alienation, insecurities, and discrimination in contrast to a vision of justice, peace, solidarity, and community engagement. This eschatological orientation invites the community to continuous action and struggle, not as a denial of the social responsibility and social transformation, but as motivation for a better future. The risks many first generation immigrants take and the hard work of many generations of Hispanics in the churches are grounded on the expectation that the future promises to be better for their children.

Contemporary developments in Hispanic hermeneutics and homiletics calls for a reconsideration of the pedagogical strategies of teaching both biblical studies and preaching. These developments echo a commitment for a solid academically and spiritually mature understanding of ministry. It affirms the importance of paying attention to the socio-historical and literary context of Scripture as well as paying attention to the social and historical context of the learning and preaching community. It promotes a study of Scripture and theology aimed not only at the attainment of knowledge, but as tools for the praxis of the struggle for liberation.

Listening and working with Hispanic in this endeavor offers benefits to the whole community. While Hispanic hermeneutics and preaching are intimately related, it is also important to call attention to the current debate on the issue of postmodern hermeneutics. In many senses Hispanic hermeneutic also shares many of the conclusions of postmodern hermeneutics. It affirms the value of feeling and intuition, assumes that objectivity is unattainable, acknowledges a degree of relativity in its view of truth, questions uncritical technological expansion, asserts the importance of the community, values tradition, and maintains that poetic language goes further and deeper than discursive scientific language. Hispanic theology is also a postmodern theology because it affirms the stories of the social and ethnic group that interprets the text.

But it is also "metamodern," as Justo L. González calls it.[9] González identifies four aspects that characterize Hispanic postmodern hermeneutics as "metamodern." (1) Most of what postmodernity suggests as an alternative to modernity and its ideology, which justified colonialism and exploitation, vindicates what the Third World, ethnic minorities, and other marginalized people have been practicing all along, recognizing and legitimizing the voices of the oppressed. (2) According to González, a "metamodern" hermeneutics is also a hermeneutics of suspicion that questions the "hidden agendas that lie behind the postmodern critique of modernity." This "hermeneutics of suspicion" rests on the Freudian psychoanalytic method that understands the behavior as manifestations of hidden, sometimes unconscious, motivations. González questions the postmodern assumption as an underlying metanarrative that there are no new narratives. (3) Although agreeing with some of the criticism of modernity by postmodern thinkers, metamodernity parts company with its proponents, understanding it as another First World way to silence and undermine

---

9. González, "Metamodern Aliens in Postmodern Jerusalem," 340–50.

the voices of the margins. (4) As interpreters and preachers of the gospel, metamodernity allows for claims in the authority of certain biblical texts to open structures of power that were created by modernity and remained unchallenged by postmodernity.

The field of the interrelationship between hermeneutics and homiletic is an open field of research and has many contributions to offer to the community of scholars and learners of the next generations. Let this first call to a table conversation be open to other voices, different voices that may challenge and question not only our assumptions but also our conclusions. Let us hope for an eschatological future where we all can learn and preach for the whole people of God.

8

Preaching John
The Word Made Flesh as Theological and Interpretive Method

KAROLINE M. LEWIS

PREACHING THE FOURTH GOSPEL has consistently been a challenge for preachers, especially within the parameters of the Revised Common Lectionary in which the Gospel of John appears as supplemental and even subsidiary to the theological and structural concentration on the Synoptic Gospels. Preachers do not know quite what to do with this gospel that is at the same time theologically rich and narratively complex. Perhaps one of the most misunderstood aspects of the Fourth Gospel that continues to have a profound effect on its preaching is the portrait of Jesus himself. There is a perceived distance about this Jesus, certainly not up-close and personal like the Jesus of Matthew, Mark, and Luke. John's Jesus is in control, orchestrating his ministry down to even his arrest.

Preaching and the Personal

This is the Jesus that carries his own cross and initiates the offer of a drink during the crucifixion with the words, "I thirst." A surreal Jesus is very difficult to preach. Where is the connection to or bond with this Jesus? How can this Jesus really be like or for us? Any personal relationship with the Jesus of John seems impossible which makes most preachers uneasy. How can a sermon on this Gospel create a real experience of Jesus when this Jesus seems to lack a sense of realism altogether? A personal encounter with the Jesus of John necessitates a way of reading John that might shed light on the profound intimacy that lies at the center of this Gospel. This essay will first set out some of the practical, literary, and theological challenges when preaching John and will then suggest an interpretive strategy so as to engage more fully John's theological framework, imaginative homiletical world, and its very surprisingly personal Christology.

CHALLENGES FOR PREACHING JOHN

Perhaps the most pressing challenge for preaching John is a practical one, namely, its role in the lectionary. As noted above, lacking its own lectionary year, John functions as a "filler" Gospel, particularly in Year B—the year of Mark, the shortest Gospel. The results of this marginalized role are threefold. First, while the lectionary does set out readings from John for several weeks in a row, there is not a consistent and sustained attention to this Gospel over the course of a year. How does the preacher best appreciate and access the narrative particularities of the Fourth Gospel when selected sections are intermittently heard and read? To what extent is the Gospel of John then marginalized in the preacher's own imagination?

Second, working within the confines of acceptable pericope length and modern chapter/verse markings, the lectionary breaks up sections of texts that belong together. A good example of this is 9:1—10:21, the healing of the man blind from birth. Perception of an abrupt change in imagery from blindness in 9:41 to shepherds and sheep in 10:1 has effectively dislodged the Shepherd Discourse (10:1–21) from its immediate context. But while the chapter ends at 9:41, Jesus does not stop talking. Although some commentators acknowledge that 10:1–21 needs to be read as the discourse following the narrated sign in chapter 9, the extent to which this informs interpretations is minimal. This is all one story within the Gospel's over all structural pattern of sign, dialogue, discourse. It is not the sign itself that is either demonstrative of Jesus' power or that which must be believed, but it is what Jesus says about the sign that is the revelatory moment. The works of Jesus are never called miracles in the Fourth Gospel. They are described as signs because they point to something about Jesus: they divulge an aspect of Jesus that this particular sign reveals. Jesus as the Word made flesh is the one who provides the words for understanding the works he does. In the lectionary, however, the passage is broken up into three separate sections over two lectionary years. 9:1–41 is Lent 4, Year A; 10:1–10, Easter 4, is always Good Shepherd Sunday in Year A; 10:11–18 is Easter 4 in Year B. The sign is separated from its discourse so that the liturgical and lectional decisions outweigh and undermine the narrative thrust and literary commitments of the Fourth Gospel.

Another challenge for preaching John is its christological portrait, as noted above. The history of scholarship on John has born witness to Clement of Alexandria's description of the Fourth Gospel as setting out to compose a "spiritual account."[1] The perception of a thoroughgoing high Christology plagues preacher and lay person alike and has proven to distance the reader from a perceived docetic Jesus. Its diversions from the Synoptic stories require the preacher to have a solid sense of the whole and to articulate faithfully its christological witness. John presents a very different Jesus from its counterparts, but difference does not have to be equated with distance. In fact, the assumed and perpetuated characterization of Jesus in the Fourth Gospel is exactly the opposite of the theological premise of the book. Preaching John becomes a pastoral issue, to

---

1 As quoted by Eusebius, *The History of the Church* 6.14: "Last of all, aware that the physical facts had been recorded in the gospels, encouraged by his pupils and irresistibly moved by the Spirit, John wrote a spiritual gospel." While this designation has had a detrimental effect in the history of scholarship for the evaluation of the historicity of the Fourth Gospel, it does point to the attributes that set it off from the Synoptic narratives.

what extent the regular preacher can afford tending and negotiating christological differences in a time of biblical illiteracy. Relatedly, a theological challenge for preaching John remains its unequivocal claim that the Word become flesh is God. The consistency with which this is worked out in the narrative places this claim directly before the listener/reader, creating an ongoing theological tension of holding fully God and fully human together all the time. This is just plain hard work.

THEOLOGICAL FRAMEWORK

It is the Gospel's very theological claim that has proven to be the bane of its homiletical existence. The prologue to the Gospel (1:1–18) contains its theological summary which not only functions as the introduction to the Gospel but suggests a methodological strategy for its interpretation. Taking this interpretive clue from the Gospel itself can provide a theology of preaching the Fourth Gospel that might inform homiletical approaches. There are several key elements of the prologue that shape interpretation of John and suggest that the Gospel itself provides its own homiletical method. Theologically, the Word made flesh puts the presence of God front and center for the experience of this Gospel. The opening claim that the Word was God leaves no question that God is revealing God's very self in every word of this story. Every sermon on John should do the same.

Preaching John means shining light in the darkness. Scholars are split as to the exact location of the moment of incarnation, 1:5 or 1:14. But if John the witness is truly a witness, testifying to the light, the light has to be shining already. John's presence in the middle of this cosmic birth story signals that witnessing is essential, not only for this Gospel, but also for its theological claim and the nature of preaching that claim. There is a necessity built into the narrative itself that that which is said here must be pointed at from outside itself. This says something about the stance and approach of the preacher when preaching John. The preacher of John stands as John the witness does, on the side, pointing to Jesus and saying,

"Look! Behold! There he is, the Lamb of God who takes away the sin of the world." For this Gospel, sin is not being in relationship with God, and the Word becoming flesh means that a deep and abiding relationship with God is possible. Homiletically, this means that the preacher asks of each and every text from John's Gospel: what does this text reveal about this relationship with God?

The word "grace" is used only four times in the Gospel of John and all in the first eighteen verses. While scholars argue convincingly for the author's use of an extant source for the prologue, such a form critical argument does not preclude using the word "grace" later in the narrative. A theological argument suggests that the rest of the Gospel is demonstrative of incarnated grace. In other words, what follows shows what grace looks like, tastes like, smells like, sounds like, and feels like. It is hardly an accident that the first sign that Jesus performs is a sign of abundant grace, water into wine. The abundance is narrated in very specific detail, six jugs, twenty-thirty gallons, filled to the brim, with the best wine. This is what grace upon grace tastes like. The homiletical assumption is that preaching John must do the same, not sermons about grace but that create experiences of grace.

Another point of entry for the prologue and John's theology of preaching is 1:18, "No one has ever seen God. It is God the only Son, who is close to the Father's heart, who has made him known" (NRSV). There are three significant facets of comparison in translations of this verse. The first is the "one and only God," *monogenēs*. Later manuscripts censor the claim by adding *son* and translations follow suit. That is, it is a lot easier to imagine Jesus, the Word made flesh, as God's son, than it is to understand the incarnation as the very real presence of a "unique God." The second difference in translations of 1:18 is the location of the Word made flesh, at the *heart*, *side*, or *bosom* of the Father. The Greek word is *kolpos*, bosom, used only here and when the beloved disciple is first introduced in 13:23. In her book, *A Complex Delight: The Secularization of the Breast from 1350–1750*,[2] Margaret Miles charts the demise of the church's primary image of God's nourishment and salvation, the image of

---

2. Miles, *A Complex Delight*.

the virgin Mary nursing the infant Christ. By 1750 with the secularization of Western civilization, the study of anatomy, and the advent of pornography, the breast was no longer a source of salvation but an object of eroticism. The image of salvation that replaced Mary nursing the infant Jesus was Mary at the foot of the crucified Christ. After 1750, there are few to no more images of Jesus being nursed by his mother, especially portraying an exposed breast.

But for the Medieval church, gazing at religious artwork was essential for faith. Physical vision was seen as a spiritual act, as art created the experience of what was being communicated theologically. Spiritual nourishment was appropriated from God to the believer. In other words, the believer was meant to imagine him or herself as the baby Jesus, and this very imagination represented, communicated, and even effused salvation. The exposed breast of Mary symbolized the nurturing God who provided believers with everything that is needed to sustain life. By 1750, the appreciator replaced the believer and art became an intellectual activity for collectors. With the gradual disappearance of the religious breast to erotic and medical associations, it became impossible to depict God's love in this way.

As a result, another central image of God's love for humanity, the cross, became the primary image. But how do you increase a physical attachment to this image as an artist? Suffering. And so, the crucifixion scene becomes suffering sacrifice as the image of God's love. This demise of the nurturing God undercuts the primary theological and homiletical claim of the Fourth Gospel, that just as Jesus is at the bosom of the Father and the disciple whom Jesus loved, the believer is as well. Everything needed to sustain life, here and now, is provided by God. This Gospel intimates that the hearer or reader of these words can imagine this abiding because the words create this experience. A narrative confirmation of this theological theme of sustenance is the presence of the mother of Jesus who bookends Jesus' earthly ministry, at the Wedding at Cana and at the foot of the cross. The sustaining and nurturing of life is taken on by the mother of Jesus when he is the Word made flesh. There is a shared nurturing, a shared parenthood, between God, the Father and the Mother of Jesus, as expressive of salvific love in the Fourth Gospel. This theological theme is reinforced by the narrative's stated purpose, "Now Jesus did many other signs in the presence of his disciples, which are not written in this book. But these are written so that you may come to believe that Jesus is the Messiah, the Son of God, and that through believing you may have life in his name" (20:30–31). While the NRSV chooses to translate "come to believe" as an aorist subjunctive, there is equal manuscript evidence to support a present subjunctive. In other words, these words are written so that you may come to believe or be sustained in your believing. This story is not information about Jesus but a means by which a relationship with Jesus is both created and nurtured.

One final homiletical cue from 1:18 is what the Word made flesh will do—*reveal, declare,* or *make God known,* all of which are fine and acceptable, especially when we think of what preaching does. The verb is *exagō,* where we get exegesis and to exegete. Quite literally, it is a compound verb that combines the preposition *ex,* "out," with the verb *ago,* "to lead or bring." The Word made flesh will lead God out. Our preaching of John must do the same, to create an encounter with the living Word where the response is, "I have seen the Lord."

The above selected analysis of the prologue to John's Gospel is meant to suggest that there are certain theological commitments of this Gospel that should guide its homiletical interpretation. In particular, the theological impulse in the prologue presents a different Christological portrait for John. While interpretations of John's Gospel continue to distance Jesus from the believer, the opposite is true when the prologue is allowed to be the interpretive lens for what follows. Against popular opinion, John's story of Jesus is profoundly intimate and personal.

INTERPRETIVE METHOD

An interpretive method that can access these critical theological issues and engage the Fourth Gospel's homiletical clues can be the concept of rereading in literary theory. I have already written on this from the perspective of secular literary theory, its use in biblical studies, and its possibility for a way of interpreting the Fourth Gospel.[3] For the purposes of this article, a brief summary will have to suffice with a specific focus on the method for homiletical implications.

Earliest descriptions of rereading are found in ancient rhetorical theory where concern for the reader or audience was of primary interest. Quintilian, for example, emphasizes for the orator the usefulness of rereading the "best" authors:

> Reading does not pass over us with the speed of a performance, and you can go back over it again and again if you have any doubts or if you want to fix it firmly in your memory. Let us go over the text again and work on it . . .We must do more than examine everything bit by bit; once read, the book must invariably be taken up from the beginning . . . the virtues of which are deliberately concealed. The orator often prepares his way, dissembles, lays traps, and says things in the first part of the speech which will prove their value at the end, and are accordingly less striking in their original context, because we do not as yet know why they are said, and therefore have to go back over them when we know the whole text.[4]

In modern, secular, literary theory, rereading is situated within reader-response or reader-oriented criticism. Reader-response criticism has been concerned with two primary questions, "who reads?" and "what is reading?" that challenge the concept of a "universal reader" and the universal goal of reading as simply a means toward an end, that is, determining textual meaning and the myth of the virginal reader. A first-time linear reading, uninterrupted and free of diversions, has become normative both for expectations of reading and reading theory, as well as the understanding of texts, and indeed, interpretation of biblical texts. Literary theorist Matei Calinescu argues that a first-time, linear reading—which typically means a "hypothetically linear reading, continuous, fresh, curious, and sensitive to surprising turns or unpredictable developments"—is a hypothetical construct because even first readings presume "a

3. Lewis, *Rereading the Shepherd Discourse*.
4. Quintilian, *Institutio Oratoria* 10.16–21.

certain degree of accuracy," and thus require "a certain amount of checking (rereading)."[5] As a result, rereading calls into question generalizations about the reader and reading, especially first-time reader constructs, linear reading paradigms, and embedded assumptions of how narratives ought to behave. Rereading corrects tendencies toward reading *only* for the meaning of a text by slowing down the movement of reading and focusing on the *process* of reading, not the *result*.

Rereading is not the same as interpretation or the *outcome* of reading, but is understood as a *process*. This assumption derives from the basic understanding that rereading is a return to a known text and thereby has an awareness of the totality of the text. When the whole of the text is taken into account, rereading has as its goal that which makes interpretation possible and not an interpretation in and of itself. This awareness of the entirety of the text realized in rereading allows for an "intercommunication" of textual features. Rereading creates multiple moments of mutual interpretive possibilities. This is essential for interpretation of and preaching on the sections of texts in the Fourth Gospel.

There are several particular literary techniques, or "textual obstacles," that impose rereading, making a first reading difficult and "messier." Texts *enact* rereading. These literary features include repetition, ambiguity, secrecy, and inherent oral features of a text. Rereading is situated within the "larger phenomenology of repetition: of remembering, revoking, reviewing in retrospect, retracing, thinking back and rethinking, rediscovering and revisiting."[6] Repetition "instantiates" rereading and gives the effect that the text is "rereading itself" by creating multiple, connecting textual moments. In particular for biblical texts, the oral elements in texts that enact rereading underscore the inherent connection between rereading and the features and functions of orality. Rereading recaptures experiences that are more akin to the "world of orality"[7] because it attends to the various "texture/s" of a text, noting the oral patterns

---

5. Calinescu, "Orality in Literacy," xii–xiii, 7, 21, 112.
6. Calinescu, *Rereading*, xii–xiii, 8.
7. Ibid., 187.

of rhythm, alliteration, assonance, repetition, antinomy and antithesis, formulaic sayings, phrasing, word sounds, onomatopoeias, rhyming, puns, equivocations, "deeper melodies and resonances" and "other auditory effects." Rereading accesses the "textualized orality" inherent in biblical texts and creates mutual interpretive possibilities between pericopes. For preaching, it is a homiletic method that starts with principles of orality. When so much of our preaching happens in the quiet and silence of our minds, tending to meaning that is grounded in the oral nature of the biblical texts captures their intended communicative response.

SUMMARY

If the fundamental narrative purpose of the Fourth Gospel, while addressed by scholars in a number of different ways, is to connect with the reader in such a way as to convince the reader of the revelation of God in Jesus Christ, and if the narrative itself invites the reader into the world of the text to be addressed by God, then there are certain literary devices at hand to achieve this goal. The theology of this Gospel is imbued in the architecture of the narrative. Therefore, rereading, and the means by which it occurs, becomes a primary way to keep the reader *in and with* the text, that is, to maintain the relationship.

One of the main reasons for keeping the reader in the text is the Gospel's theological theme of "abiding." The use of *menō* in the Gospel is a primary term for the believer's relationship with Jesus. The relationship into which Jesus invites his followers is not "sporadic," but one that reflects his own relationship with his Father and the Spirit.[8] This relationship is, in part, the response of faith that is not "a one-time decision, but develops over time"[9] and is an "ongoing process." The phenomenon of rereading is a means by which to ensure that this very personal relationship is both ongoing and "permanent" at the breast of the Father.

---

8. O'Day, *The Gospel of John*, 531.

9. Reinhartz, *Befriending the Beloved Disciple*, 56–58.

By creating a way to experience the Gospel and its revelation that can be shared by both the community for which it was written and present-day readers, the Gospel once again brings to fruition one of its major theological themes and homiletical premises: the presence of the Word in the world even after Jesus' return to the Father. Rereading invites the present-day reader to "come and see," just as did the first disciples. Moreover, the mutuality of relationship between texts that is brought to light by the strategy of rereading becomes a narrative device that serves to emphasize the relationship into which the Gospel bids the reader. In a related manner, the rereading of the Gospel becomes the mode by which grace upon grace (1:16) can occur, and the abundance of all that Jesus provides is perpetually realized in the repetition of the Word. In this sense, a strategy for reading the Gospel of John that attends to its "self-referring quality"[10] is essential, not only for the sake of its essential theological claim, that God is fully present in Jesus Christ, but also for the way in which this Gospel wants to create the experience of abiding.

One final way in which the idea of rereading highlights theological themes in John, especially for preaching, is in reference to time and the eschatological framework of the Fourth Gospel. Rereading both accesses and accentuates the "hymnic 'eternity' and narrative 'temporality'" of a Gospel that represents an "intersection between eternity and time."[11] That which is offered by Jesus in this Gospel, for both the characters whom Jesus encounters and its readers, is not a future possibility but a present reality. This collapsing of the expansion of time into a moment of response from the believer is captured in the process of rereading. Rereading is at the same time looking forward and looking backward so as to come to a momentary understanding of the present. Rereading captures this tension between the "both/and" of the present and future and emphasizes the experiential nature of the Gospel text, thereby reinforcing the existential moment for the reader,[12] the hearer of

10. Meeks, "The Man from Heaven in Johannine Sectarianism," 68.

11. Thompson, *The Struggle for Theology's Soul*, 110–11.

12. Dewey, "The Gospel of John in Its Oral–Written Media World," 251. The use of "existential" here focuses on the "experience of the performance

the sermon, and the timed timelessness of the preaching event. As Käsemann notes, "John's eschatology . . . no longer emphasizes the end and the future, but the beginning and the abiding."[13] It is an eschatology that is in service to the incarnated Word, and in particular informs a theology of preaching that keeps you in that Word. Rereading as interpretive methodology makes possible the abiding that this Gospel wants, that its theological premise demands, and that preaching on John's Gospel should create in each and every sermon.

SERMON: *LOVE YOU FOREVER,* JOHN 19:26-27[14]

The crucifixion of Jesus in the Gospel of John is really quite short. Eight verses, to be exact. Sure, there's a lot that happens before the actual crucifixion—the arrest, the trial, Jesus carrying his own cross to Golgotha. And there is a lot that happens after—the piercing of Jesus' side, Scripture being fulfilled, his burial. But the crucifixion itself is only eight verses long. And in those eight verses, it turns out, Jesus has a lot to say. Three of the seven last words of Jesus come from John's Gospel, including "I thirst" and "It is finished." But his very first words from the cross? "When Jesus saw his mother and the disciple whom he loved standing beside her, he said to his mother, 'Woman, behold your son.' Then he said to the disciple, 'Behold your mother.' And from that hour the disciple took her into his own home." As Jesus is dying, we are reminded of who gave him life. As he is crucified, Jesus reminds us of who he really is. Yes, the Word made flesh. Yes, the great "I AM." Yes, the one and only God. But when he sees his mother, he asks us to see her, too. And in seeing the mother of Jesus, we are reminded that he was and is also us. Human. Flesh and blood. A man who was once a boy, who had a mother. And who is the one you need when you know your life is

---

event, not on the specific information being learned or reinforced," 246.

13. Käsemann, *The Testament of Jesus,* 20.

14. This sermon was delivered Good Friday, April 6, 2012, at Central Lutheran Church in Minneapolis, Minnesota.

ending? Who is the one person you want with you when you know you are dying? Well, for Jesus, here and now, it's his mother.

From the cross we hear the words, "Behold the lamb of God who takes away the sin of the world." Behold; look; see. From the cross, Jesus sees the disciple whom he has loved, whom is never given a name, at the foot of his cross, there *with him* and *for him*, as he is dying. And, he sees his mother. His mother, whom *we* have not seen since the wedding at Cana, way back when in chapter two. The mother of Jesus, never named Mary in John's Gospel, appears only at the wedding at Cana and the foot of the cross. In her presence here, now, at the moment of her son's death, we see that she has surrounded Jesus' presence in the world. Her love for her son brackets Jesus' life for the world. His love for her is what he needs to say before he leaves this world.

She was there at the beginning. Jesus' first miracle. His first sign. His first big moment. I wonder, if it weren't for her, would that miracle have happened? She's the one who points out to Jesus, "they have run out of wine." Jesus' response? "Woman, what concern is that to you and to me?" or, to put it in today's terms, "Mom, I kinda think that's their problem. Bad planning. They should have hired a better wedding coordinator."

Yet, she's the one that encourages him. "Come on, come on, you can do it." The thought that comes to my mind is the time I was standing at the bus stop when my youngest son got on the school bus for the very first time, the first day of kindergarten. Thinking, and then saying out loud, "Come on, off you go, you can do it!" Now, I know, getting on the school bus and turning water into wine are not the same thing; certainly not on the same level of miraculousness. But I do wonder if it's the same kind of feeling of being a mother. It doesn't matter what your child is doing for the first time: walking; climbing the rock wall at the playground; first day of preschool; a piano recital; the first middle school dance. And so, at the very first thing that Jesus does—being Jesus, even when he is the Word made flesh, the light in the darkness, the Lamb of God—well, his *mom* is there, prodding him, pushing him, saying to him, "you can do this." Maybe, in that moment, Jesus finally sees that he can.

He needs his mother to tell him. To believe in him. To see what he can do and to see who he is.

Of course, obviously, *this day, today, on the cross,* is a different kind of moment. This is no beginning. These are not first steps. This is the end. The last steps. And here, now, Jesus needs his mother again. To see him for the last time, maybe to say again for the last time, "you can do this." But then, the proverbial tables are turned. In a way, they need to be turned, have to be turned. Jesus sees her. For the mother she has been. For the mother she still needs to be.

One of my favorite children's books that I read to my two boys more often than I can count is called, *Love You Forever* by Robert Munsch—which, since 1986, has sold more than 15 million copies. It tells the story of a mother and her son. When the son is a baby, the song that she sings to him goes like this, "I'll love you forever, I'll like you for always, as long as I'm living my baby you'll be." The baby grows up, of course, becomes a two-year-old, a nine-year-old, a teenager, and then a grown-up man. At each stage of his life, she sings him this same song, holding him, rocking him. When she is old, too old and too sick to sing to him or to hold him, he holds her and sings the song to her, "I'll love you forever, I'll like you for always, As long as I'm living, my Mommy you'll be."

Now, when the tables are turned, Jesus sees his mother. Sees her for what she has been for him. Sees her for who she is. Sees her for what she needs to continue to be. He makes sure that she is taken care of. He makes sure that she is provided for. He makes sure that she can continue to be a mother. "Behold *your mother,*" Jesus says to the disciple whom he loves. Jesus' words to his mother on the cross are this promise: "You have been my mother, you are my mother, and you need to be a mother. Here is your son. And I'll love you forever."

And today, in this word from the cross, Jesus says, "Behold, I see you. I see who you are, who you want to be, and who you need to be." Because, while seeing is most certainly believing, believing is seeing, seeing the relationship with God that Jesus makes possible for us, today and on Easter Sunday. Today you are seen for who you have been, for who you are, for who you want to be, for who you need to be, but now for where you need to be, with God, forever and always. And here's the thing. There is nothing quite like that feeling. There is nothing quite like that kind of relationship. There is really nothing quite like that kind of love.

9

Scholars and Soccer Moms
Reflections on Objectivity and Subjectivity in Moving from Text to Sermon

CHARLES L. AARON

A MARINE BIOLOGIST AND an artist look at the ocean differently. A marine biologist asks questions about the ecosystem and the interrelation of species within that system. This approach to the ocean proceeds by collecting and interpreting data, with a goal of accuracy. An artist sees the beauty and power in the ocean, ruminating on the ways it evokes metaphors about the unknown or the expanses we cannot traverse, with a goal of insight. I do not know enough about marine biology or art to know if a painter and scientist can learn anything from each other. I do know, however, that pastors and scholars approach biblical texts in different ways. I write this essay as part of an ongoing dialogue about how the two approaches can work together in the service of preaching.

An exact delineation between the two approaches proves elusive. Preachers approach texts with individual idiosyncrasies while scholars have developed an ever-accumulating array of methods for reading texts. Part of the problem involves the complexity of biblical scholarship and the lack of consensus in the academy about what one does when one reads and studies the Bible. Understandably, busy parish pastors find the assimilation and mastery of these methods intimidating. Describing the difference between a pastoral approach and an academic approach to reading texts cannot avoid generalizations. In broad strokes, scholars ask about such things as what the text reveals of history, the evolution of religious thought, or the rhetorical goals of the writers. Preachers ask questions about the normative value of the text, the ways it might provide guidance, empowerment, and comfort for contemporary communities of faith. Describing the difference between the two approaches runs the risk of oversimplification. Some preachers make extensive use of the academic methods; some professors write for the church. As an example of scholarly efforts to speak to the needs of the church, see such commentary series as *Feasting on the Word*, *New Interpreter's Bible*, and the *Interpretation* series. Still, a great deal of scholarly work proceeds without concern for the religious needs of the church.

Much twentieth-century scholarship advances from the university-influenced goal of bringing the humanities to the same level of academic rigor as the natural sciences. Biblical scholars wanted to produce verifiable results, leading to historical-critical methods and positivism.[1] The late twentieth-century and early twenty-first-century have seen the development of postmodern approaches that appreciate the narrative quality of texts and the ambiguity of biblical research.[2] These developments have produced a dynamic field of

---

1. See Lemche, *The Old Testament between Theology and History*, 33.

2. See the entry, "Postmodern Biblical Interpretation," in Soulen and Soulen, *Handbook of Biblical Criticism*, 140–42. That article points out that "postmodern biblical interpretation contends that the meaning of a text is not 'in' the text waiting to be recovered through the use of neutral, generally applicable criteria. Rather, textual meaning is constructed through the interplay of a text's semantic and rhetorical aspects and the reader's own life-world."

research and conversation, but may seem impenetrable to a parish pastor.[3]

Preachers, sometimes even with impressive academic credentials, approach a text for preaching in different ways than scholars. An examination of the written reflections on the sermon writing process by prominent preachers provides one type of access to the ways preachers approach texts. A concern for the effect of the sermon on the congregation serves as an overarching goal of preaching. As Zan Holmes, pastor emeritus (although recently having come out of retirement as interim pastor) of St. Luke's United Methodist Church in Dallas, TX, writes, "I believe that the major task of the preacher is to enable the Word of God to happen again for the preacher and the congregation."[4] This aspiration for the sermon bears some similarity to the goal of the artist in painting the ocean: to have a visceral impact on those who view the painting.

In seeking to draw out of the text insights that will enable a visceral impact of empowerment, comfort, and conviction, a preacher often approaches a text in an intuitive way, rather than the deliberate way a scholar approaches a text. As an example of this intuitive approach, Barbara Brown Taylor describes her method of exploring a text for preaching: "My own [routine] begins with a long sitting spell with an open Bible in my lap, as I read and read and read the text. What I am hunting for is the God in it, God for me and for my congregation at this particular moment in time."[5] The quality Taylor seeks seems difficult to define with precision. She admits to a lack of control in the process and draws an analogy with electricity to describe how it works. This analogy speaks to the visceral effect of the text within the preaching process. She carefully includes a step in her process of determining the "original meaning" of the text, pairing her intuitive reading with the scholarly methods. One can characterize her overall method as intuitive because she suggests that the "God" in the text strikes her on a level other than the cognitive. She seems to describe a kind of "aha" moment when she

---

3. See Adam, ed., *Handbook of Postmodern Biblical Interpretation*, for a description of the leading methods of postmodern interpretation.

4. Holmes, "Enabling the Word to Happen," 74.

5. Taylor, *The Preaching Life*, 80.

finds the "God" in the text, a moment that she recognizes, but that another reader/preacher might not replicate.[6]

Even though the complexity of contemporary biblical studies and the lack of evidence about how preachers approach texts make the exact delineation of the differences difficult, one can say that biblical studies, both in the academy and in the parish, move between two poles: objectivity and subjectivity. Although one of the goals of the historical-critical method was a kind of objectivity in biblical studies—the attempt to discern the original meaning of a text—postmodern biblical studies question the role of objectivity in the approach to texts. I want to suggest that for certain questions the goal should be to examine the text with as much objectivity as one can muster. I will define the term "objective" as the attempt to study the text as an object. Through critical analysis, what can one determine about the text concerning how, when, and why it was written? By subjective I mean the process by which an interpreter of scripture recognizes that she or he brings assumptions and life experiences to the tasks of exegesis and study. As an example of the goal of objectivity, I cite an explanatory comment by David Noel Freedman in Raymond Brown's *An Introduction to the Gospel of John* in the Anchor Bible Reference Library. Describing the goals of the series, Freedman asserts, "the approach is scholarly, the perspective is balanced and fair-minded, the methods are *scientific*."[7] As an example of subjectivity, I again cite Holmes, who explains, "I find it necessary to exegete myself before I exegete the text."[8] Scholars, of course, have recognized that issues of gender, class, social location, and ethnicity affect biblical studies.

Even though scholars and preachers share the task of reading the Bible, each might see the ways the other approaches the task as

---

6. Both Taylor and Holmes have academic credentials and have taught seminary. Their approach is not anti-intellectual in any sense, but seeks both a visceral/spiritual impact as well as intellectual integrity. The scholar typically proceeds without concern for this visceral/spiritual impact on a community.

7. Brown, *An Introduction to the Gospel of John*, no page number, but this comment comes at the very front of the book, right after the title page, emphasis added.

8. Ibid., 75.

unhelpful. Preachers might say that the results of scholarship do not help them appropriate the text for proclamation. Effective preaching involves enabling an impact in the congregation that touches intellectual, emotional, and spiritual levels within the hearers. The "scientific" approach sought by Freedman might not achieve this result. A scholar might say that the process described by Holmes and Taylor lacks precision and standards for verification.

An important contribution to the ongoing conversation about engaging a text of scripture in preparation for preaching is the book by Anna Carter Florence, *Preaching as Testimony*.[9] From an academic perch, she explores the process by which a preacher taps into her or his life experience while studying a text. After recounting the history of women preachers who preached passionately, Florence enumerates in the last part of the book several exercises by which contemporary preachers can explore a preaching text in creative and intuitive ways. She tends to turn nouns into verbs in this part of the book. The title of this chapter derives from one of the exercises, where she encourages preachers to "soccer mom" a text.[10] When I first read that section of the book, I mused about how one could incorporate both academic methods of study with "soccer momming" a text. The rest of this chapter represents my attempt to answer my own internal question.

To explore the issues of objectivity and subjectivity, I will take a rich text, John 12:1–11,[11] and use four methods to examine it with an eye to the preaching possibilities. Because a form of this passage appears in all four gospels, it lends itself to a variety of methods of academic study. Because it is a powerful and dramatic text, with a strong woman character at the center, it lends itself to subjective reflection. I will use two traditionally accepted academic methods, one diachronic and one synchronic, to examine the text. These

---

9. Florence, *Preaching as Testimony*.

10. A preacher "soccer moms" a text by writing the pericope on an index card and asking another spectator at a soccer match to say what the text means to her after reading the text from the card. This process provides a spontaneous insight into the text.

11. The limits of this text are often considered to be verses 1–8, but the continued mention of Lazarus leads me to continue on to verse 11.

methods are redaction analysis and narrative analysis. Then I will use two of Florence's methods, one communal and one individual, to examine the text. I will report the results of "slanging" the text with the youth at Whaley UMC and the results of "imaging" the text in a quiet place alone.

The incident recorded in John 12:1-11 has connections with two stories in the synoptic gospels, one told by both Matthew and Mark and one told by Luke (Matthew 26:6-13; Mark 14:3-9; Luke 7:36-48). In Mark (and the Matthew parallel), an unnamed woman pours expensive oil over Jesus's head while he eats at the home of Simon the leper in Bethany. In Luke, an unnamed woman enters the home of a Pharisee in Galilee. Identified as a sinner, the woman weeps on Jesus's feet and then wipes them with her hair, kisses them, and pours oil on them. Raymond Brown describes a plausible historical reconstruction of two incidents from the ministry of Jesus that stand behind these accounts.[12] During Jesus's Galilean ministry, a penitent sinner weeps on Jesus's feet and then, because of embarrassment, wipes his feet with her hair. In the second incident, a woman anoints Jesus's head with oil while he is in Bethany. The writers of the synoptic gospels record these incidents, with Luke adding the anointing to his story of the weeping on Jesus's feet. John combines elements of these narratives and changes the context, identifying the woman as Mary, Lazarus's sister.

Theologically, the three accounts (considering Mark and Matthew as similar enough to constitute one account) serve different theological purposes. In Mark, the incident takes place near the time of Jesus's burial. The significance of the story lies in the possibility that it will strengthen the proclamation of the church as it preaches in the world. The story serves the evangelism of the early church. In Luke, the incident leads into a parable about sin, guilt, forgiveness, and gratitude. The story bursts the bubble of self-righteousness and exhorts the church to open its doors to all who truly repent. By changing the context and the identity of the woman, John places the emphasis on worship. Mary expresses gratitude to Jesus, not for forgiveness, but for the return of her brother. By having Judas

---

12. Brown, *The Gospel according to John I-XII*, 450–51. Brown cites the research of Benoit and Legault.

protest insincerely about the lack of charitable giving, instead of asking honest questions about why the expensive perfume was not sold for charity, John uses the story to critique hypocrisy and the unwillingness of Judas to believe, even in the face of incontrovertible evidence (the presence of Lazarus). Mary performs a spontaneous act of devotion, given gratuitously, celebrating resurrection as both a future promise and current experience.

A researcher can legitimately set a goal of objectivity in this use of redaction criticism. One can marshal arguments about possible historical incidents that lie behind the narrated accounts. This part of the process involves conjecture, and the results are not assured, as Brown acknowledges that some scholars assume a single incident lies behind the accounts. Issues of forgiveness, gratitude, belief, and worship are not inherently "objective" topics, but one can look at these accounts with the goal of objectivity to discern how John uses previous material, and some of the ways he want to use the stories passed on to him. One draws conclusions from examining the text, not from reflection on one's own experience. A researcher's sex, ethnic identity, or social location should have minimal influence on the conclusions drawn about how John has redacted this narrative. Another researcher might disagree about the emphasis John places on worship in this pericope, but that researcher would marshal objective arguments about that issue.

Commentators have offered copious praise for John's skill as an author. John's characters, even given their brief appearances, display complexity, embodying some aspect of what it means to believe or not believe. The conversations in John, which seem not to follow logical conventions of conversation, push the theological reflection to a deeper level. A full-blown narrative analysis of this passage would yield much fruit. For the purposes of this essay, a few comments will have to suffice. This part of the story works by setting up a series of contrasts. Lazarus represents life while Jesus's opponents plot his death. The aroma of the perfume contrasts with the presumed smell of death in the previous chapter (11:39). Mary's generosity exposes Judas's selfishness. Her genuineness confronts his hypocrisy. Lazarus and Mary both remain silent, allowing their presence and actions to provide their witness. Judas's words conflict with his internal attitudes and future actions.

As Susan Hylen points out, Mary represents an ambiguous character. Throughout chapters 11 and 12, Mary displays both faith and unbelief. She expresses belief in Jesus's healing power and ability to prevent death (11:32), but she does not dialogue with Jesus as Martha does and ends up simply crying, a response of grief. In chapter 12, she anoints Jesus with the expensive perfume, but Jesus interprets her actions. In Hylen's words, "Mary's ambiguity lies in the reader's inability to determine with any certainty what she understands about her own words or actions. Yet Jesus's words impart to Mary's actions a deep sense of his ministry and purpose. His interpretation and the later event of his death add meaning to Mary' act of anointing Jesus's feet, no matter what she understands about her actions."[13]

I would argue that narrative criticism combines objective and subjective stances toward the text. A researcher asking narrative questions objectively looks for clues in the text about how the author has shaped characters, set up conflict, composed dialogue, employed literary devices. On this level, researchers can seek to resolve disputes about conclusions by appealing to evidence. Nevertheless, how one responds to a narrative involves subjective elements. Identifying with a character may depend upon the life-situation of the reader. The emotion evoked in a reader by a narrative may depend not upon evidence, or the intentions of an author, but on the circumstances of that reader.

As a parish pastor, I see a connection between both the contrast inherent in the passage and the ambiguity of Mary's level of belief and worship. Genuine worship is marked by generosity, risk-taking, gratitude, affirmation of life, and devotion—the qualities Mary displays in contrast to some of the other characters in the story. Although worshippers obviously use words, actions play a significant role in worship, as Mary's silent actions do in the narrative. Worship always involves actions, the significance of which the actors do not fully comprehend, as with Hylen's insight about

---

13. Hylen, *Imperfect Believers*, 86–87.

Preaching and the Personal

Mary's role in the narrative. The actions in worship carry significance only because God receives and incorporates those actions into a larger picture. As Hylen comments about Mary's anointing of Jesus, "But Jesus breathes into them a life that goes beyond the limitations of her intentions. Regardless of her own intentions, Mary's actions come to embody the fullness of Jesus's action in the raising of Lazarus."[14] Such in-breathing takes place in worship as well.

Florence's book is an important contribution to biblical hermeneutics for preaching with historical, theological, liberative, ethical, and creative dimensions. At least the third part of the book is an examination of the subjective element in the process of exegesis. Any attempt to summarize the book will naturally oversimplify it. In advocating for the subjective element in biblical hermeneutics, she calls for a deep, risky immersion in the text. She wants preachers not only to use their own experience in the hermeneutical process, but to engage the text in a deep, transformative way. She recognizes that her process involves risk, both in the act of reading and in the bold preaching that she hopes will result from this reading. In relating her advice to students, she writes, "What I don't tell them—not right away then, anyway—is that every sermon kills you. For me, the act of preaching is really an act of dying. But it is also the act of being raised by the power and grace of God. This Word we preach takes us with it all the way to the cross and all the way back."[15] She clearly affirms that this deep personal engagement with the text does not allow for a fully subjective treatment. In her words, "One very important reiteration: this does not mean that anything goes as far as Scripture is concerned and that we can mold the biblical text into anything we want to say."[16]

In the third section of her book, Florence offers a list of exercises that she advocates for her students. These exercises carry the potential to enable the goal articulated by Taylor and Holmes, of finding the "God" in the text for a particular situation and allowing the text to create an experience in the preacher that the preacher

14. Ibid., 87.
15. Ibid., 130.
16. Ibid., 84.

can then recreate in the congregation. For this essay, I have chosen two of the exercises: Image it and Slang it. She divides the exercises up into "Exercises for Attending" and "Exercises for Describing." Attending to the text is "a way of being, seeing, and living in the text and in the world and its primary task is to receive in openness."[17] Describing involves "finding words to express what we have seen in our attending."[18] She lists "Imaging" the text as an exercise in describing; but as I read her summary, I understood it more as a way to attend to the text than to describe what one has seen in attending. Imaging the text calls for the preacher to write a list of images in the text, close one's eyes and allow oneself to "see" the words and pictures that come up. After opening the eyes, one writes down everything one's inner mind saw when the eyes were closed. This process seems to me to be more a way of seeing in the text than describing what one has seen. A preacher "slangs" the text by rewriting the text in the idiom of youth or young people.[19]

I performed the exercise on four images in the text: table, jar, hair, and feet. When I imagined the table, I saw people sitting around it. The table provided structure. A table can connote power or community. I tried to imagine Lazarus sitting at the table and what types of facial expressions he might have after his experience. I guessed he might have a look of serenity on his face, as though he knows something others do not. I wondered if food tasted different after death and reanimation. I wondered why John gave us no tearful reunion scene between Lazarus and his sisters. Lazarus himself never speaks in the passage; all of the other characters react to him. So, this exercise gave me the opportunity to focus on him, to imagine him as a character.

When I imagined the jar of perfume, I wondered how Mary handled it. I assumed she would be careful with it. I wondered if she hesitated before she poured out the perfume or if she charged right into it. I wondered how she walked toward Jesus: boldly or timidly. She is not a bold character, so I guessed she might have

---

17. Ibid., 135.
18. Ibid., 143.
19. These exercises are described on 146–47.

walked in timidly to perform her act of devotion. I imagined her heart pounding in the process.

In imagining Jesus's feet, I suspected they were rough and calloused. Even after appropriate cleaning, they were likely stained. This image of Jesus's feet added to a sense of the earthiness of Jesus, especially in a gospel in which Jesus often appears otherworldly.

I imagined Mary's hair as unruly, not perfectly coiffed. I assumed it was long and flowing. Mary's hair made me think of femininity and vulnerability.

This experience did help to vivify the text. In keeping with the theme of worship, it brought to mind the vulnerability and uncertainty with which we worship.

When I performed the exercise of "slanging" the text with the youth of my church, I discovered that they had a hard time seeing the incident as a gestalt, to where one scenario would fit every element of the story.[20] We came up with a series of dynamic analogies for the various parts of the story. The incident takes place at Pentecost, but they considered Christmas a time they associate with experiencing God's presence. When I asked them how youth would express the presence of Lazarus at table as living sign of Jesus's identity as light, truth, and life, they said that "legit proof" would be a contemporary expression. An act comparable to pouring out the expensive perfume in devotion might be giving up a cell phone, but more likely selling one's car and giving the money to the church.[21] The aroma of the perfume expanding to fill the room reminded them of hearing on mission trip about all the food they had collected and how many people it would feed. In reflecting on Judas's hypocrisy, they thought of trying to be a typical rebellious, experimenting teenage, while also wanting to be a Christian and making a contribution to the church. Although Judas raises his question about giving the money to the poor insincerely, his concern is legitimate. How does

---

20. The youth who participated in this exercise included Lindsay Biffle, Mallory Case, Anna Beall, Josh Garcia, Tony Mason, Melodie Vavra, Chelsea Vavra, Jamie Eddleman, and adult leader Kelley Crawford.

21. An article on the internet tells of church youth who gave up money raised for a ski trip to feed those who are hungry. Nunn, "Teens Sacrifice 'Want' To Meet Needs."

one adjudicate between worship and service/justice ministries? They saw this conflict in youth who participate in mission trips, but never attend worship. Service to the poor matters, but so does worship.

If I add up the results of using these four approaches to this passage, I can affirm some ways that they work together. Redaction criticism suggests that John has taken two accounts that originally supported the church's evangelism or an understanding of sin and forgiveness and focused it on worship. Narrative analysis highlights the ways that our actions in worship mean more than we realize. Jesus's death and resurrection give significance to our actions in worship. Worship includes risk, generosity, and affirmation of life in the midst of cynicism and death. Reflecting on the images in the text enabled me to concentrate on the uncertainty we bring to worship. In wondering about Lazarus's experience, or Mary's emotions in her actions, I realized that we worship with mixed motives. The exercise with the youth gave me insights into their world, and how they understand sacrifice, gratitude, hypocrisy, and worship.

I want to suggest two contributions for this essay. First, the academic methods can generate ideas for sermons. They do not just provide boundaries for the preacher's imagination. Second, Florence's section on methods for attending to the text lists "study it" last.[22] She implies, but does not state, that study comes last in the process. I want to make explicit that study and the use of the academic methods comes both before and after the use of the imaginative, intuitive methods. Attending to the redaction, structure, and internal workings of the text facilitated the use of her methods. The more a preacher can know about the text on the front end, the more useful these intuitive methods will be. Objectivity in studying the text facilitated the subjective experiencing of the text.

Neglect of either objectivity or subjectivity in studying texts leads to problems in preaching. Exegesis that leans too heavily on subjectivity can allow the preacher to overwhelm the text. The text cannot "defend itself," so to speak. If both preachers and scholars understand hermeneutics as a conversation, then the text has a

---

22. *Preaching as Testimony*, 143.

word to speak in the conversation. A diligent attempt at objectivity on the part of the interpreter allows the text to speak its word, even if that voice travels across languages, time, and distance.[23] As an example, I have heard sermons on the David and Bathsheba story that described the event as either a seduction on Bathsheba's part or a rape on David's part. The text itself does not explain what actually happened in the bedroom or Bathsheba's motives for taking a bath (other than physical cleanliness). The power relationships throughout the story are complex (see 2 Sam 11:1–5). David L. Bartlett explains the problems with placing too much emphasis on the critical methods (not exactly equated with objectivity in this essay, but the remarks still illuminate the problem): "My own sense is that preaching these days is less apt to suffer from a surplus of imagination than from a lack of imagination. I do not know that I want us to sin boldly, but I want us to preach a little more boldly. We are so scared of allegorizing and psychologizing that we may be afraid of mattering. We get it all right, every exegetical jot and tittle, but what does it matter? Whom does it save?"[24]

Scholars and preachers can learn from each other. Even the most careful marine biologist can appreciate the beauty of the ocean. Scholars seem aware that the methods they use do not open the text to the visceral impact a sermon needs. Preachers seem aware that the academic methods at least provide boundaries beyond which their imaginations and intuition cannot go. Preachers may find themselves more attracted to the subjective methods, but the academic study provides integrity to the task of preaching. An artist can paint a picture of the sea with a mermaid breaking the surface of the water, a detail not supported by the scientific study of marine biology. A preacher, however, ought not to go beyond the boundaries set by careful scholarship. Working within the

---

23. As Clark-Soles asserts, "Modernist approaches are beneficial in that they force us to draw out and honor the original meaning of the text in its original context so that we don't simply make the texts mean whatever we want them to mean." She goes on to describe the contribution of these methods as providing "a spectrum of more and less reasonable interpretations, better and worse." *Engaging the Word*, 23.

24. Bartlett, *Between the Bible and the Church*, 29.

boundaries of the academic methods can channel the imagination of the preacher. A worthy goal for the balance of objectivity and subjectivity in approaching texts would be preaching marked by disciplined creativity.[25] The use of subjective imagination provides the creativity, while the academic methods push the preacher toward disciplined objectivity.

SERMON: *WORSHIPPING ONE LORD IN GAINESVILLE, TEXAS*[26]

I rejoice in the opportunity to come together as Christians during the season of Lent. The body of Christ has divided itself so hopelessly that I can't imagine we ever will come back together fully on this side of the resurrection. Nevertheless, I still rejoice that we can share this meal and this time together. Theology divides us, but I can live with that. We can share a faith, but still debate theology. I can handle the fact that John and his Calvinist flock are correct to place so much emphasis on the sovereignty of God, but wrong about predestination [John Hare serves as pastor to First Presbyterian Church in Gainesville, Texas]. Just so you know, I graduated from a Calvinist seminary, so I hope I can joke with the Calvinists! I grieve more that worship divides us. The sacraments serve as one example. The sacraments should unite us, but they divide us more deeply than theology. You can find a Methodist on nearly every side of any theological issue even at Whaley, but we don't let those disagreements keep us from eating the body and drinking the blood of Christ together. So, we can get past our theological differences for the sake of worship. We cannot seem to bridge the chasm that worship creates for us. When we practice baptism, the rite that initiates us into the faith, we find ourselves hopelessly divided. We can't even agree on what to call the other sacrament—the Lord's Supper, Communion, the Eucharist—much less how to practice

---

25. Cf. the term "imaginative precision" that Ellen Davis suggests in *Wondrous Depth*, 68.

26. This sermon was presented at the community-wide 2012 Lenten Luncheon Series in Gainesville, Texas.

it. Who can distribute the elements? Who can receive them? That sacrament sustains and nourishes our faith, but separates us from one another.

What can we learn about worship from the Gospel of John? Of the four gospels, John treats the sacraments in the most understated way. John gives only the briefest description of Jesus's baptism. At the last supper John describes a foot-washing, not a communion service. For John, the sacraments peek out at us from the background. Even this passage here does not explicitly mention worship. John tells us about a scene that sounds familiar from the other gospels. Mark tells a story about a woman who anointed Jesus's head with expensive ointment, but Mark puts the emphasis on evangelism—wherever anyone proclaims the word, they can include this story. Luke tells of a woman who wept on Jesus's feet and dried them with her hair, but that story teaches us about forgiveness—her many sins had been forgiven. John's story sounds a little like them, but not quite. If we compare John's story to the other gospels, we see that John tells a story that teaches us indirectly about worship.

Jesus has raised Lazarus, the brother of Mary and Martha, from his tomb. Jesus *is* the resurrection and the life. Mary can't contain her gratitude to Jesus for restoring her brother to her. We can probably imagine Mary, a rather quiet woman, timidly standing up, clutching the jar of ointment, determined to do what she felt led to do. Who knows why she passed by Jesus's head to anoint his feet, but she did. Did her shyness get the best of her? Whatever her reason, she poured out the expensive perfume on Jesus's rough, calloused feet. With everyone seated around the table, with the meal proceeding the way the host planned, Mary's act disrupts the order, the structure of the evening. All of a sudden, everything changes. When Mary anoints Jesus's feet, that act draws the lines. On one side of the line stands Judas, who shows his greed and hypocrisy. On the other side of the line stands Mary, who gives generously. On one side of the line stands Lazarus, who represents life. On the other side of the line stands the religious leaders, who plot Jesus's death. On one side of the line stands Mary's silent actions, on the other side of the line stands Judas's insincere outburst. On one side of the line stands the stench of death from the previous chapter, on this side of the line stands the aroma of Mary's perfume that fills the house.

The perfume fills the house. Mary starts at Jesus's feet, but what she does moves outward, expanding, filling up space, going beyond what she expected. She started small, but watched her efforts fill the whole house. We rejoice that God takes our efforts and uses them for things we never imagined. When our youth go on mission trips, they like to hear just how many lives they touched, in ways they never expected. God takes our small efforts and fills the house.

Mary's act may have started small, anointing Jesus's feet, but her act showed great generosity. She anointed Jesus's feet with expensive perfume. She didn't give what she had left over after taking care of everything else; she gave the best she had. The average Protestant gives two percent of his or her income. Mary used the expensive perfume. Mary makes me think of the youth group from Amarillo, who raised money for a ski trip, but ended up giving the money to feed the hungry instead.

Mary must have given the perfume out of a sense of deep gratitude and wonder over her brother. We don't know much about why she grabbed that perfume, interrupted the dinner party, and poured it all over Jesus's feet. We don't know exactly why she let down her hair and wiped them. We kind of assume that the gratitude just welled up inside her. She felt a gratitude she couldn't contain.

If John doesn't tell us why she did what she did, he does tell us this much. She did not know the full significance of what she did. She acted in gratitude and then Jesus interpreted it. Jesus told her and everyone else that her act prepared him for burial. She acted in gratitude and Jesus gave her actions meaning.

We all will remain brothers and sisters in Christ, but we will never overcome all of our differences. Yet, as we read this story together, can we see some things that will scoot us a little closer together? Can we see that at the heart of worship we all share a sense of gratitude to God for life and for God's victory in Jesus over death? Can we see that when we worship we perform actions that we do not fully understand yet? Can we see that in worship we do things that have meaning because of what God does with those actions? In this season of Lent, let us offer worship to God, who understands what we do not. With all the divisions among us, let us find common ground in grateful response to God, who sent us Jesus as the resurrection and the life.

10

Hearing the Voices of Others
A Collaborative Reading of Leviticus 19

J. DWAYNE HOWELL

IN 2003, I PARTICIPATED in a group presentation at the annual meeting of the Southeastern Commission of the Study of Religion in Chattanooga, Tennessee. The topic of discussion was, "Responses to 9/11." My paper, titled "An Understanding of the *gēr* in Leviticus 19:33–34 and the Treatment of the Immigrant," dealt with the rise of xenophobia in the United States after the attack of 9/11 and the appropriate response to the immigrant (*gēr*). The tragedy of 9/11 has been compounded by the rise in hate crimes against those citizens of foreign birth or ancestry. Especially affected by this rage are those of Middle Eastern descent.[1]

---

1. Monteith and Winters, "Why We Hate," 44. Monteith notes in her article that within five months of the September 11 attack over 1,700 cases of abuse were reported against Muslims.

Preaching and the Personal

As I began to rework the paper for another research project, I came to the following realization: "Who am I to write on such a topic?" I have never been an immigrant in a strange land. Instead, I am a white Anglo-Saxon Protestant raised in a middle class family and I am steadily employed as a college professor. Through this discovery, I began to wonder what others see in the passage. Not only should my imagination be a part of hearing the text, but the imagination of others likewise should be heard. My research led me to the area of collaborative preaching,[2] which seeks to include the voices of others in studying the text. Closely related to the study of collaborative preaching is the area of Contextual Hermeneutics, which seeks a cross-cultural listening to the text. From this research, I developed a study guide that I used in three different Bible studies. The following is a summary of my research. I have included a synopsis of the Leviticus 19 passage, background on collaborative preaching and contextual hermeneutics, and responses from the Bible studies.

SYNOPSIS OF LEVITICUS 19:33–34

Gēr is used ninety-six times in the Old Testament with twenty-two of those occurrences in the book of Leviticus, five times in vv. 33 and 34.[3]

Leviticus 19:33 and 34 states:

> When an immigrant resides with you in your land, you shall not oppress the immigrant. The immigrant who resides with you shall be to you as the citizen among you, and you shall love the immigrant as yourself; for you

---

2. McClure, *The Round-Table Pulpit*; Atkinson, *Sharing the Word*.

3. Kellerman, "*gur*," 442. Kellerman notes that *gēr* is used altogether 36 times in the Priestly source and 22 times in Deuteronomy. Thus, over half of the occurrences of the word occur in the Pentateuch (58 times). See also Meek, "The Translation of *GER* in the Hexateuch and Its Bearing on the Documentary Hypothesis," 172–80. Meek shows a development of the concept of *gēr* in the first six books of the Old Testament. It could mean "immigrant" (one entering the land), "resident alien" (one settled in the land), and "proselyte" (one who has adopted the ways and culture of the people of the land).

were immigrants in the land of Egypt: I am the LORD your God.[4]

An overarching concept in the Old Testament is that the *gēr* was a foreign-born resident who had migrated to Israel. This designation seems to cover a large range of people. Biblical evidence shows that the Israelites were not the only people to leave in the Exodus (Exod 12:38). Joshua's address to the people at the covenant renewal ceremony at Shechem suggests a wider variety of people present than just the Israelites.[5]

Not only were there those who were from other countries and backgrounds involved with Israel in the Exodus and the Conquest, there would also be the normal migration of non-indigenous people into Israel. This migration could arise for various reasons.[6] First, there is the natural movement of people in and out of the region.[7] Today, as well as then, groups of semi-nomadic and nomadic people travel throughout the region. A second reason for migration would arise out of natural causes such as drought, famine, and disease. These frequently occurred in the ancient Near East leading to mass migration of people groups looking for food and relief.[8] A third

4. The passages are quoted from the NRSV. I have chosen to translate the Hebrew *gēr* as "immigrant" instead of "stranger." The Hebrew word *gēr* is translated variously as "sojourner" (BDB), "alien," or "resident alien"(NRSV, REB, NAB, NJB, NIV), and "stranger" (KB, RSV, KJV). The noun is based on the verb *gûr*, "to sojourn" or "to tarry as a sojourner." *Gēr* conveys both the idea of a "temporary dweller" and a "new-comer who had no inherited rights since he would not be related to those in the community or tribe." The *gēr* is not seen as a "foreigner" (*nakrî*); instead he or she resides in the land but is not a native of the land

5. In Josh 24:14–15, Joshua addresses the people as those who are "from beyond the River" (Mesopotamia), those who dwell in the land (Canaanites/ Amorites), and those who once worshiped the gods of Egypt. Those present would not just be Israelites, descendants of Abraham, but would also be representatives from other peoples groups.

6. KB, 1:201. See also Kellerman, "*gur*," 443.

7. Abraham refers to himself as a *gēr* (Gen 15:13; 23:4).

8. Two examples found in the Old Testament are Joseph's changing situation in Egypt (Genesis 43–50) and the story of Ruth. In the story of Ruth the reader is first told of Elimelech taking his wife, Naomi, and sons, Mahlon and Kilion, to Moab from Bethlehem during a time of famine. Likewise, Ruth, who

reason for the migration of people would be the constant warfare in the lands of the ancient Near East. Refugees would commonly search for peaceful areas to settle. Finally, people would migrate to escape from crimes and the vengeance of others.[9]

Using the background of the migration of persons and whole groups, an appropriate definition for *gēr* would be "immigrant." Immigrant is defined as "a person who comes to a country to take up permanent residence."[10] On the one hand, terms such as "stranger" and "sojourner" emphasize the lack of local identity, but do not suggest the permanence that an immigrant may experience in the land. On the other hand, terms like "alien," "foreign-born resident," or "resident alien" speak to one's permanence in the land, but can be derogatory, and the latter ("resident alien") is considered an oxymoron.

Leviticus 19 addresses how the less fortunate are to be treated by the Israelites. All dealings with the people of the community were to be based on justice and no partiality toward the rich or the poor was to be shown (v. 15).[11] The less fortunate are described in a variety of ways in Leviticus 19:

- vv. 9–10—poor and immigrant (in the collection of gleanings from the fields)
- v. 13—laborer (payment of daily wages)
- v. 14—the deaf and the blind (against mistreatment)
- vv. 20–22—the female slave (protection)
- v. 29—the daughters (not to be sold into prostitution; cf.

---

is a Moabite, is also a widow and an immigrant in Israel when she returns with her mother-in-law Naomi. She even partakes in the practice of collection "gleanings" as prescribed for the poor and immigrant in Lev 19:10).

9. Exod 2:11–22. See also Exod 18:3. Here Moses explains the name of his son Gershom (*gēršôm*): "because I have be a sojourner (immigrant) in a foreign land" (*kî . . . gēr hāyîtî bĕ'ĕrĕs naākĕrîyāh*).

10. *Webster's New Collegiate Dictionary*, 573.

11. DeVaux, *Ancient Israel*, 1:73. DeVaux notes that in the prophets the rich are grouped with other influential people and political leaders who faced prophetic condemnation. The poor, though, are seen as individuals who were isolated and defenseless because they were not a part of a social class

Deut 23:17)
- vv. 31–32—the elderly (due respect and honor in society)
- vv. 33–34—the immigrant (concerning his or her treatment in the land)

Those included in the list would be among the most vulnerable in the community.[12] They could easily be taken advantage of by unscrupulous people in the community. Especially vulnerable would be the immigrant who would have neither property rights nor family ties to rely on for protection. Thus, the Israelites are encouraged to care for the less fortunate in their community.

If the *gēr* is viewed as an "immigrant," he or she is not just passing through the land but is seeking to settle in the land. The admonition to care for the poor and neglected of one's own social group, as well as one simply "passing through" the land, is found in the writings of the ancient Near East. Such hospitality was an important part of everyday life in the ancient Near East. Unlike our concept of hospitality today (clean sheets and one's bed turned down with a complimentary chocolate on the pillow), hospitality in the ancient Near East was a matter of life and death.[13] However, the call to care also for the immigrant who is *settling in the land* appears to be unique to the literature of the Bible.[14] As with the

---

12. Two groups not included in the list in Lev 19 but are common in other passages about the less fortunate are the "widows" and "orphans." See also Gowan, "Wealth and Poverty in the Old Testament," 341–53.

13. Malina, "Hospitality." Malina's article deals primarily with the New Testament concept of hospitality, but is also applicable to its practice in the ancient Near East.

The practice of hospitality in the ancient New East is still being carried out in the Middle East today. The lifestyle of the Bedouin peoples provides insights to the practice of hospitality in the Middle East today. Lughood, *Veiled Sentiments*. The author, a woman, describes her travels in Bedouin groups and their various practices, including hospitality. Bailey, *Bedouin Poetry from Sinai to the Negev*. This book contains several Bedouin poems that deal specifically with hospitality.

14. Gowan, "Wealth and Poverty in the Old Testament," 343. Instructions to care for the poor citizens in one's community can be found in the Code of Hammurabi, ca. 1700 BCE. See also Peterson, "The Widow, the Orphan, and the Poor," 226. Such instructions can be found in the Egyptian Instructions of

poor, disabled, widows, and orphans, the immigrant could easily be taken advantage of in the land. The immigrant entered the land both homeless and landless.[15] In order to survive, the immigrant would often become indebted to another and end up a slave to that person.

Israel is reminded that they were once in a similar situation as the immigrant in their land. The time spent in Egypt has a twofold significance for Israel. First, their ancestors had migrated to Egypt during a time of famine while Joseph was a leader in Egypt (Gen 46:1—47:28). However, once they had settled in Egypt after the time of famine, a Pharaoh came to the throne who "did not know Joseph" (Exod 1:8) and oppressed the Israelites in Egypt (Exod 1:9—2:25). Israel's ancestors in Egypt experienced both the hospitality of Egypt in time of need and the tyranny of Egypt during a time of servitude.

Exodus 22:21 and 23:9, as well as Deuteronomy 10:19, parallel Leviticus 19:33-34. In these passages, Israel is likewise reminded that it had sojourned in Egypt. Exodus 23:9 states that the Israelites know the "heart" of the immigrant because of their time in Egypt.[16] In *A People Called: The Growth of Community in the Bible*, Paul D. Hanson sees the early community of Israel as "living in memory" of the Exodus.[17] Central to that memory would be God's compassion in the act of deliverance. Hanson believes that this memory should lead Israel to practice "compassionate justice." Thus, the Egyptian

---

Amen-em-ope, ca. 1250–1000 BCE. See Oden, ed., *And You Welcomed Me*, 17.

15. Pohl, *Making Room*, 28. Pohl notes that immigrants were "landless in an agrarian society where land was usually distributed by inheritance and where access to land was essential to life."

16. Each of the passages in Exod, Lev and Deut are found in the three major codes of the Pentateuch: The Covenant Code (Exod 20:22—23:19, one of the oldest Israelite legal codes); The Deuteronomic Code (Deut 4:44—26:8; 28:1–68); and the Priestly Code (Exod 25:1—Num 10:10). Martin-Achard, 'gwr, 309. Martin-Achard dates the references as follows: Exod 22:20b is the oldest, followed by Deut 10:19, and finally Lev 19:34. He views Lev 19:34b as developing from Deut 10:19.

17. Hanson, *A People Called*, 45. In this section Hanson is actually dealing with Exod 22:20b and its relation to the Covenant Code.

sojourn reminded the Israelites of the importance of hospitality for the ones who would now sojourn in their land.[18]

BACKGROUND ON COLLABORATIVE PREACHING

I have the opportunity to serve as a part-time pastor as well as a professor. I have been associated with my current pastorate for over twenty years, first serving as a student pastor (1984–1991), and then returning as pastor in 2001. I consider the members to be my family and know many of their life stories. As I became more and more aware of these stories, I wanted to know what they were thinking about the text I preached each Sunday and how they viewed the text's implications. I longed to hear the voices of the others. Concerning such a "view from the pew," Lucy Rose Atkinson observed: "I remember how often I have listened to a preacher describing what 'we' do or feel or think, and I was aware that the statements might reflect the preacher's reality but they did not reflect mine; 'I' was not included in the preacher's 'we.'"[19] Atkinson called for conversational preaching, preaching that allowed for both the "particularity and the diversity of other experiences."[20] John S. McClure names this type of preaching "collaborative preaching." In his book, *The Round-Table Pulpit: Where Leadership and Preaching Meet*, he defines collaborative preaching as "a method that involves members of a congregation in sermon brainstorming."[21] He advocates moving from a "sovereign style" of preaching, which is centered on the preacher offering the final word, to a "working together" between the minister and the listeners. Out of this collaboration, the sermon emerges.[22] McClure offers both the theory and the practical

---

18. In several biblical passages the Israelites are reminded that they are still strangers/sojourners in the land because the land belongs to God (Lev 25:23; 1 Chron 29:15; Pss 39:12 [Heb. v. 13]; and 119:19).

19. Atkinson, *Sharing the Word*, 127.

20. Ibid.

21. McClure, *The Round-Table Pulpit*, 7.

22. Ibid., 48.

application of collaborative preaching in his book. He encourages the inclusion of a broad range of people in the conversation about the text. However, he also emphasizes that the pastor needs to be an active part of the discussion and offer his or her own "instructive 'otherness.'"[23]

I have also found in my research that the field of Contextual Hermeneutics is closely related to the ideas found in collaborative preaching. Often, Contextual Hermeneutics are applied to cross-cultural views of the text.[24] However, Daniel Patte provides an introduction to the use of Contextual Hermeneutics in a small group setting in his book, *The Gospel of Matthew: A Contextual Introduction for Group Study*.[25] The study guide provides for the small group to meet three times.[26] The purpose of the first meeting is to share the various contextual interpretations of the passage of each group member. The second meeting compares the contextual interpretation with interpretations of the text from scholarship, sermons, and the arts. The final meeting seeks to provide an appropriate interpretation of the text for the present and the application of the text to a concrete situation.

RESPONSES FROM THE BIBLE STUDY

I did not duplicate McClure's or Patte's models entirely in my research. Instead, I chose several settings to conduct the Bible study on Leviticus 19 in order to gain a variety of perspectives. These settings included a rural church, a multi-racial urban church, a group of international college students, and personal conversations with international missionaries. The rural church is located in central Kentucky. It was founded in 1801 and includes Thomas Lincoln, Abraham Lincoln's father, among its early membership. The church had also taken an early stand against slavery. The small membership

---

23. Ibid., 54.

24. For more information about this cross-cultural use, see Segovia, *Decolonizing Biblical Studies*; and Dietrich and Luz, *The Bible in a World Context*.

25. Patte et al., *The Gospel of Matthew*.

26. Ibid., 12–14.

is made up primarily of professionals and retired persons who have strong ties to small farms. The urban church is set in a metropolitan area of approximately 270,000 people. The urban church is situated in a changing community and is currently in the process of developing a multi-racial ministry to involve the diverse population of its neighbors. This church also took a strong stand for civil rights during the 1960s. The international student group is part of a larger international student body at a private Baptist-affiliated university in central Kentucky.[27] The university has one of the highest per capita populations of international students of the private colleges in Kentucky representing 35 countries. I interviewed three missionaries in my research. The first was a retired missionary who served as a seminary president in Africa. The next two, a couple, served as missionaries in Central America. They served primarily with the Guaymi Indians in Costa Rica and surrounding areas.

I sought a mixture of age, gender, and, when possible, race in each group. The groups consisted of eight to ten participants to allow for opportunity for all to be a part of the discussion. I developed a study guide that was used in all three settings based on the work of Daniel Patte. Each individual participant was provided with the study guide to prepare ahead of time and to be used in the group discussion. The guide consisted of the following instructions and questions:

Indicate translation used

1) Read Leviticus 19:18, 33–34.

2) Write these verses in your own words.

3) Describe a current situation that applies to the text (this can be personal or it can be a current event).

4) What is the basic need that you see in the situation you described (i.e. family, work, community, cultural, etc.).

5) Re-read the text. How does it address the need in the

---

27. The international students did not commit as readily as the other groups. Various reasons for this include: commitment at times is difficult due to responsibilities; lack of information; lack of understanding of the format of the study. Two students from Japan did come to the Bible study and provided their insights.

situation you described?

6) Now read all of Leviticus 19.
7) How does Leviticus 19 further address the need that you have described?
8) What have you learned from the text?
9) Is there a question that you have that has not been addressed?

The study guide did not provide exegesis of the passage, but was primarily intended to help each person express his or her thoughts about the text. I then met with each group for a one- to two-hour discussion about the text. It was during this time that I provided exegetical information about the text in the form of a brief introduction, and then as questions arose during the discussion.

The following is a summary of the group responses:

Translation Used

The translation used by most participants was the New International Version (NIV). Other versions included the King James, New Living Translation, Living Bible, and New Century Version. I provided the NIV translation of the passage for the international students but also encouraged them to read it in their own languages if a translation was available.

Write in Your Own Words

By allowing the participants to write the passage in their own words, it provided an opportunity for me to see what ideas and concepts stood out to them in the verses. Many emphasized the forgiveness and love one is to show another. Some, but not all, included the call to love the immigrant because we, too, were at one time immigrants.

Describe a Current Situation

In describing a current situation that applies to the text, some shared personal circumstances including interpersonal relationships. One, a retired school teacher, noted how she had observed how new students would often be ostracized by other students.

The dominant response in both the rural church and the urban church was to the current situation in the United States involving immigration. This topic, by far, took a majority of time in the discussion. Some referred to the migrant workers as the "Mexicans" (though many are not from Mexico but from other Central and South American countries). Migrant workers are present throughout the state of Kentucky. They provide labor in agriculture, restaurants, and the horse industry. Note was made also of the increasing population of Japanese in the state. Many of the Japanese in Kentucky are affiliated with Toyota Manufacturing and its subsidiary companies around the state. However, the discussion centered on the treatment of and the response to the migrant worker population in the state.

Two important issues emerged in the discussion in the rural church, primarily centering on the migrant farm workers. The first issue concerned the legal problems many migrant workers face. Several of the members of the rural church serve in a capacity in the court system. Often, their contact with migrant workers is when certain laws have been broken or the court system is abused. This, they admitted, affected their views on immigration. As I discussed the situation with the church members, we noted together that I had contact with immigrants primarily who are in the United States to continue their education and often do not enter the court system.

A second issue emerged concerning migrant farm workers. One person stated that his opinion concerning immigration is affected by the use of migrants for cheap farm labor on large "corporate farms." He believed that this was a contributing factor to the decline in the number of small family farms since they are unable compete with the cheap labor.

However, the discussion also included the treatment of the immigrants who are often forced to live in sub-standard conditions on limited pay. Also, they are taken advantage of by unscrupulous people. The problem is compounded if they lack the ability to speak English.

In the discussion with the international students, the comment was made by one Japanese student about prejudice in her own culture. It mainly centered on the relationship between Japanese and Koreans. When she came to the states she realized the prejudice she had developed as she became acquainted with other students who were Korean. Over time she became good friends with those students.

What Is the Basic Need in the Situation That You Described?

As the discussion continued, I found that the participants often discussed the need along with the response to the need found in the biblical passages. The basic need that many shared was dealing with fear. Fear for the immigrant and fear for themselves. As mentioned, most people knew of the unfair treatment of many migrant workers. Many noted the need for kindness and understanding for them. One suggestion was the offering of assistance, including English as Second Language (ESL) courses. One person even mentioned the need for SSL courses (Spanish as a Second Language). The urban church had in place other methods of offering assistance through both the church and local community organizations. Both the rural church and urban church voiced frustration over what to do for a need that seemed so overwhelming.

Fear of the immigrant was also something they felt they needed to confront. Underlying the concern of many regarding immigration was the sense of fear that many had of those entering the country, especially after 9/11. Added to the fear of the migrant worker, several noted their fear of those of Middle Eastern dissent or Muslim tradition.

An interesting story was shared by one member of the group from the urban church. He was an African-American who had met resistance from a Caucasian neighbor when he moved into a new house. He stated that he dealt with the problem with kindness and over time his neighbor became accepting of him.

The missionary couple who worked with the Guaymi Indians in Central America noted a strong prejudice among the Costa Ricans toward those of neighboring countries, including Guatemala and Nicaragua, as well as toward the Guaymi Indians.

How Does the Text Address the Need?

The participants saw the text addressing the situation in several ways. At this point more participants began to reiterate that we were strangers in this land at one time. Emphasizing God's example of unconditional love, the consensus of those in both the rural and urban church was that everyone should love, support, and respect each other.

The sharing of hospitality was emphasized in several groups. The retired missionary from Nigeria had ample opportunity to travel throughout the country in his role as a seminary president. In going from village to village he noted that proper protocol was expected. This meant always asking permission from the tribal chief and elders before entering a village. Once invited to enter, he was under the hospitality and protection of the tribe. He stated that such hospitality was common throughout the culture. However, he noted that Nigeria is composed of many tribal groups and tensions are present among the various groups over territory. For such a reason, hospitality plays an important role in the culture.

How Does Leviticus 19 Further Address the Need that You Have Described?

When the participants responded to reading Leviticus 19, many began to make broader applications of the text. Noting the slogan of Wal-Mart, "Always the Lowest Price," one participant in the urban church stated the slogan had a dark side and that the low prices come at a cost: underpaid and overworked laborers both in the United States and abroad. Seeing the call to take care of not only the immigrant but also others less fortunate in society, the question was asked: "What are we willing to sacrifice?"

Frustration became evident in the discussion in both the rural church and urban church as the participants began to realize the full ramifications of the text. One summed it up with the question echoed by many: "What is the answer?"

At this point in the discussion I encouraged the participants to present specific ideas for their churches to reach out to the immigrant. The urban church had already begun to adopt strategies for become a multi-racial church. Included in their ideas were the ESL and SSL programs mentioned earlier. They also began to discuss strengthening their greeter ministry, which is used to welcome visitors to the church. One of the participants said that in order to breakdown barriers he often begins with the statement, "Tell me your story." The rural church spoke of a need for some of the local ministers associated with the United Methodist Church. These ministers are not from the United States and are having difficulty retaining permission to remain in the country. Part of this is due to the stricter immigration laws since 9/11.

What Have You Learned from the Text?

In sharing what they had learned from the study one comment stood out: "Nothing is said (in Leviticus 19) about our receiving a blessing in return." I had missed this myself in my studies of the text. The instructions for the faithful in the chapter are simply to be obeyed without concern about what is received in return. These instructions are accentuated throughout the chapter with the reminder, "I am the Lord," or, "I am the Lord your God."

Is There Any Question You Have That Has Not Been Addressed?

I purposefully included the last question, "Is there any question you have that has not been addressed?" in order to allow the participants to respond with questions that I had not thought about in my own research. One person, in the rural church, asked a question about the instructions concerning raising fruit and breeding animals found in verses 19 and 23-25. This is a perfect example of how people are drawn to topics in the Bible that interest them. The woman is from a farm family and she was interested in the reason for these instructions in Leviticus 19. Her question provided an opportunity for another Bible study on the text of Leviticus 19.

Two questions that are very important were included on the study guide, but the participants asking them did not bring them up in the discussion. First, one asked if we are still called upon to follow the book of Leviticus. That the Old Testament is superseded by the New Testament is a common view in the church. Leviticus is viewed as containing outdated regulations that are no longer required. Such views highlight the need for a further understanding of the Old Testament's relationship to the New Testament. The Old Testament's view on the treatment of the immigrant and the less fortunate is echoed in the New Testament. Also, while certain ritual regulations found in Leviticus may seem outdated, its instructions concerning the meaning of being the people of God, especially as found in the Holiness Code (chs. 17—26), are still important guides for interpersonal relationships.

A second question a participant asked from the study guide was: "If we are to treat the immigrant/stranger as a citizen, what are we to do if they have come here to do us harm?" This once again stresses the fear sensed by many in both the rural and the urban churches. No mention is made in the Old Testament concerning the response to a stranger who may harm another. In ancient Near Eastern practices, one was to offer hospitality even to an enemy if requested and the enemy was to be given a three-day head-start before the host could pursue him. A comment related to this second question was made in the rural church. The belief was that society as a whole was safer in biblical times than it is today and people more readily take risks. However, several biblical stories emphasize the dangers strangers faced traveling in the ancient Near East and their reliance on the hospitality of others for protection (cf. Genesis 19; Judges 19; Luke 10:29-37).

CONCLUDING REMARKS

The topic of immigration is an important issue in the United States today. The events of 9/11 and the work on immigration reform in the Congress places the subject on the minds of many in the church. Leviticus 19:33–34 provides a paradigm for the treatment of the immigrant. The Israelites were to treat the immigrants with fairness, compassion, and as fellow citizens. The reason for this emerges out of God's own gracious acts toward Israel in delivering them out of being immigrants in Egypt.

Through the use of collaborative reading of the Leviticus passage, others were given voice to share both their thoughts and fears concerning the text. That this was a pertinent subject for today was seen in the eager participation in the open discussion. The participants voiced opinions and questions concerning the text. While I played a role in moderating the discussion and adding exegetical notes, both groups shared and offer self-correction to one another on various issues that were raised. The consensus of both the rural and the urban church was that all people needed to be loved, cared for, and protected. However, frustration was seen in both settings because the task seemed so daunting for a local church to accomplish. Through brainstorming, each group began to develop plans for applying the text to their context. Even though the groups agreed that the immigrant is to experience compassion and that the local church can address the issue, fear proved to be a major obstacle for the people to overcome. The fear centered on what the immigrant might do in return.

Several personal observations emerge from the collaboration on Leviticus 19. First, churches and individual missionaries gladly entered in to the study. However, students did not commit as readily. Various reasons for the lack of commitment include: commitment at times is difficult due to responsibilities; lack of information; and lack of understanding of the format of the study. Still the amount of information received in the Bible studies and groups was overwhelming and could not all be incorporated into one sermon. Instead, it has provided a basis for an ongoing conversation on the treatment of the stranger.

Another observation is that I already had predetermined outcomes in mind of how the study would conclude. One is that the international students would be able to teach us true hospitality. Actually, many of their cultures mirrored the American tendencies in offering hospitality.

I also had a concern about how to deal with disagreements in the group. However, I noticed that each group that I worked with had an ability to be self-corrective without my entering into the discussion.

The collaborative reading of the text provided for me a better insight into its application by listening to the voices of others. I learned from the participants where they are in the text. They also pointed out topics that I myself had missed in my studies. I do not view collaborative reading/preaching as diminishing my role as a pastor. Instead, it provides for me the opportunity to better understand those to whom I minister.

SERMON: *RESPONDING TO THE STRANGER*[28]

Text: Leviticus 19:33–34; Matthew 25:31–46
We are in the twenty-third week of ordinary time, the time between Pentecost and Advent. For twenty-six weeks, we consider our response to the gospel story that is celebrated between Advent and Pentecost.

—Birth, Life, Death, Resurrection of Jesus
—The empowerment of the church

What does all of this mean for us? How should our lives be changed by our remembering these events?

This sermon is a culmination of what we have been doing this year: trying to understand how we respond to the stranger. We have incorporated a new method of Bible study. I have also led this study with other churches, international students, and missionaries. I

---

28. This sermon was preached at the Rolling Fork Baptist Church in Gleanings, Kentucky, on Sunday morning, November 4, 2007. It is specific for the congregation and includes material from both personal research and the collaborative Bible studies.

wanted to hear the voices of others, not just my own voice, on the subject.

How Do We Respond to the Stranger?

Leviticus 19 reminds us that we are to treat them as one born in our land, to love them as ourselves. It is in direct parallel with Leviticus 19:18: "You are to love your neighbor as yourself." Jesus illustrated Leviticus 19:18, who is our neighbor, in the story of the Good Samaritan. Our neighbor is anyone that we meet, regardless of race, creed, or origin of birth.

There are many strangers in our land, immigrants from other countries. A major debate in Congress (and in the public) today is what to do with the mass number of immigrants coming in to the United States. At any given time in the world there are 150 million immigrants, those displaced from their own land. Why? Some are part of a natural movement of people. Others seek to escape drought, famine, disease, or natural disaster. Warfare displaces many. Still others seek to escape from persecution or crime. Most of the 150 million immigrants are not seeking to bring chaos in the lands to which they migrate; they are simply seeking a better life. These are the most vulnerable in the world's communities. They have little, if any, family connections, no property rights, and limited knowledge of the land's language and customs.

Now place yourself in the same situation. If, for some unforeseen reason, you became homeless, how would you fare in another country? How much time would you have to learn the language and customs of a new land—*when you are trying each day to earn enough money to feed yourself for that day?*

Lest we think that the immigrants in our land are simply freeloaders, let us remember that we all benefit from their labors when we check out at the grocery. One comment made in the Bible study concerned Wal-Mart's "Always Low Prices." This comes with a dark side: The low prices come with a cost—*underpaid and overworked laborers, at home and abroad.* Would we be willing to make the same sacrifices for those who make sacrifices for our comfort?

These are the people that we do not often see or think about, *unless they become a perceived threat to our way of living.*

Are We Still Responsible for the Requirements That Are Found in Leviticus 19?

Simply put—*Yes*! The ethical requirements found in Leviticus 19 are found throughout the Old Testament and are also found throughout the teachings of Jesus. Matthew 25:31–46 tells the story of the separation of the sheep and the goats, the separation of the righteous and the unrighteous: "When did I see you hungry or thirsty or a stranger or needing clothes or sick or in prison?" *If God was to separate us out today, where would we be?* Note that in this passage salvation is based on action or inaction in meeting the needs of those around us. This is not a salvation of works, but action that emerges from our relationship with Jesus Christ. Look at what Jesus has done for me! Think about it—*grace abounding*! The proper response to such grace is to share it with others.

What Stops Us from Sharing Such Grace? Not Knowing What Will Happen and Not Knowing What to Do

Not knowing what will happen is often based in our fear of the unknown. Most participants in the Bible studies expressed this emotion. We live in a post-9/11 world—fear is a part of our culture. *Is the one that I will help a terrorist*? Most likely not. Our sister church, Highview United Methodist Church, knows first hand that not every immigrant presents a danger. A beloved former pastor, Brother Doug, was from Canada. Yet, he knew from experience the problems with immigration, facing the threat of deportation not because he was a threat but because his visa was expiring.

Fear can paralyze one into inaction. *Fear that is not dealt with can lead to hatred.* It should also be noted that in the texts today nothing is said about our own safety in offering hospitality. Hospitality involves discernment on our part; discernment based on our relationship with God and with others. As Matthew 10:16 reads,

"I am sending you out like sheep among wolves. Therefore be as shrewd as snakes and as innocent as doves."

The second reason many do not share the *abounding grace* is because they do not know what to do. As one person wrote, *What is the answer*? It just overwhelms us when we think of the magnitude of this challenge. One other thing to deal with in our lives:

> What is going on in our personal lives?
> What is going on in our own community?

Several think we need to take care of those at home first. We are tempted to move in to a protection mode, a cocoon to protect us from the world. But even in a small church like ours, what we can do affects others around the world. Have you ever noticed roses in the fall season? Most roses bloom, showing life and the potential for life. Still, some blooms never open up. They actually turn in on themselves, die, and rot. The same is true for churches and the possibilities of *abounding grace*. So, what type of church will we be? A church that opens up to the possibilities that God places before us? Or a church that turns in on itself and dies?

Is There Something We Can Do?

David Coffey, President of the Baptist World Alliance, speaking at Campbellsville University, shared about his travels throughout the world and seeing the needs throughout his journey. He shared how it can be an overwhelming task to try to meet all the needs. However, in his challenge to the students he stated: "God has not called us to do everything, but God does call us to do something." I offer you two opportunities to do something. These opportunities are intend to begin the process, not to limit it. First, provide a meal at the university one night during the holidays for the international students. Many cannot go home and have no other place to stay. Also, the cafeteria on campus is closed. It involves a one-night commitment to feed the group. Second, be an International Friendship Family and adopt an international student during the semester. This allows your family to get to know another by inviting a student over for dinner, providing a periodic retreat for them from the hustle and bustle at school, and inviting the student to special events with your family. When I told Susan about this she said this would be a wonderful experience for any one of you based simply on our experience with you over the years.

These are simple ways to begin to open the door to responding to the stranger. What is something that you can do? I pray that this will be a new opportunity for us to share our experience of *abounding grace* with others.

11

Epilogue

J. DWAYNE HOWELL

THE BIBLE, THE SERMON, and the congregation are all intricately related to the personal. Each is influenced by what is seen and heard and by how events and words are interpreted. The biblical text has a rich historical context in the ancient Near East that aids the reader in understanding what the text meant. However, this history is not a static history, locked in the past. Instead, it is a dynamic history of the divine acts of God that can be seen throughout the canonizing process as successive generations interpreted the tradition and text for their situations. The interpreted history has continued throughout the ages and continues even today as the minister steps in the pulpit and proclaims, "Thus saith the Lord." There is a sense of the divine present in the reading and interpretation of the text as many traditions share in the confession, "The Word of God for the People of God," responding, "Thanks be to God." The words are not limited to the text or the sermon, for many seek to understand what it means to be the People of God in the world.

The interpreted history of the Bible often does not offer a single meaning for the text, but multiple meanings. Questions including historical and sociological context, literary form, rhetorical purpose, and cultural/contextual hermeneutics open possibilities for new understanding of the text. These possibilities challenge both the minister and the listener theologically and culturally. There are inherent risks in challenging the status quo and long held beliefs. Two of those risks are rejection by others and a misperception of the meaning of the text. These two points underline the need for an ongoing dialogue about the text between the preacher and the listeners. This can be accomplished through what Ellen F. Davis calls the "confessional" reading and teaching of the Bible in the church, "the need for the church to learn afresh to acknowledge the Bible as the functional center of its life, so that in all our conversations, deliberations, arguments, and programs, we are continually reoriented to the demands and promises of Scriptures."[1]

Two of the elements to confessional reading that Davis discusses apply directly to preaching and the personal. The first is reading the text with theological interest.[2] This begins with the reader's awareness of God and self and their interrelatedness. This is accomplished, according to Davis, by a slow reading of the text to appreciate its literary artistry. Ruthanna B. Hooke in her chapter provided a basis for studying the text using performance theory. Karoline M. Lewis spoke to the importance of the personal in the Gospel of John. Chuck L. Aaron offered a close reading of John 12:1–11. These essays spoke of the importance of the biblical texts and the minister's role in interpreting the text.

Davis' second element emphasizes that the reader has to be open to repentance, a change of mind: "Because the Bible speaks with multiple voices, it attests to the perpetual struggle of the faith community to test different perspectives."[3] Anna Carter Florence calls the reader to boldly speak even though others may see his or her words as idle speech (*leiros*). In his essay, "The Risk of

---

1. Davis, "Teaching the Bible Confessionally in the Church," 9.
2. Ibid., 10–16.
3. Ibid., 16.

Testimony," Walter Brueggemann reminds the reader that "Witnessing can become as jaded, routine, and trivial as every other mode of discourse. Its lively urgency depends upon the recognition of the high stakes of the contestation."[4] The chapters by Valerie Bridgeman Davis and David Cortés-Fuentes concerning Womanist hermeneutics and Hispanic preaching make us aware that the congregation is as culturally diverse as the world and provide differing perspectives for interpretation. Finally, John S. McClure's and J. Dwayne Howell's chapters on collaborative preaching encourage ongoing conversations with others, inside and outside the church, so that they also can have the "opportunity for a community to both *perform memory* (in a Bible study), and then to witness *memory in performance* (in the sermon and liturgy)."[5]

Preaching is personal. It must listen to all who bear testimony to that fact.

---

4. See Brueggemann, "The Risk of Testimony," 55, above.
5. See McClure, "Collaborative Preaching and the Bible," 69, above.

Appendix
Hispanic Biblical Hermeneutics and Homiletics: A Brief Bibliography

DAVID CORTÉS-FUENTES

Aponte, Edwin D., and Miguel de la Torre, editors. *Handbook of Latina/o Theologies*. St. Louis: Chalice, 2006.
Arrastía, Cecilio. "La Iglesia como Comunidad Hermenéutica." In *Voces: Voices from the Hispanic Church*, edited by Justo L. González, 122–27. Nashville: Abingdon, 1992.
———. *Teoría y práctica de la predicación*. Miami: Caribe, 1978.
Cortés-Fuentes, David. *Mateo. Conozca su Biblia*. Minneapolis: Fortress, 2006.
———. "Sin." In *Handbook of Latina/o Theologies*, edited by Edwin D. Aponte and Miguel de la Torre, 91–97. St. Louis: Chalice, 2006.
Costas, Orlando. *Comunicación por medio de la predicación*. San José, Costa Rica: Caribe, 1973.
———. "Evangelism from the Periphery: A Galilean Model." *Apuntes* 2 (1982) 51–59.
———. "Evangelism from the Periphery: The Universality of Galilee." *Apuntes* 2 (1982) 75–84.
———. *Liberating News: A Theology of Contextual Evangelization*. Grand Rapids: Eerdmans, 1989.
———, editor. *Predicación Evangélica y Teología Hispana*. Miami: Caribe, 1982.
Crane, James. *Manual para Predicadores Laicos*. El Paso, TX: Casa Bautista de Publica-ciones, 1966.
———. *El Sermón Eficaz*. El Paso, TX: Casa Bautista de Publicaciones, 1961.

Appendix

Croatto, J. Severino. *Biblical Hermeneutics: Toward a Theory of Reading as the Production of Meaning.* Maryknoll, NY: Orbis, 1987.

De La Torre, Miguel A. *Doing Christian Ethics form the Margins.* Maryknoll, NY: Orbis, 2004.

De La Torre, Miguel A., and Edwin David Aponte, *Introducing Latino/a Theologies.* Maryknoll, NY: Orbis, 2001 [esp. 71–77].

Elizondo, Virgilio. *The Future is Mestizo: Life Where Cultures Meet.* Bloomington, IN: Meyer-Stone, 1988. Rev. ed., Boulder: University Press of Colorado, 2000.

———. *Galilean Journey: The Mexican American Promise.* Maryknoll, NY: Orbis, 1983. Rev. ed., 2000.

———. *Mestizaje: The Dialectic of Birth and Gospel, a Study in the Intercultural Dimension of Evangelization.* 3 vols. in 2. San Antonio: Mexican American Cultural Center, 1978.

Espín, Orlando O., and Miguel H. Díaz, editors. *From the Heart of Our People: Latino/a Explorations in Catholic Systematic Theology.* Maryknoll, NY: Orbis, 1999.

Fernandez, Eduardo C. *La Cosecha: Harvesting Contemporary United States Hispanic Theology (1972–1998).* Collegeville, MN: Liturgical, 2000.

———. "Reading the Bible in Spanish: U.S. Catholic Theologians' Contribution to Systematic Theology." *Apuntes* 14/3 (1994) 86–95.

García, Alberto L. "Christian Spirituality in Light of the U.S. Hispanic Experience." *Word & World* 20/1 (2000) 52–60.

García-Treto, Francisco. "Crossing the Line: Three Scenes of Divine-Human Engagement in the Hebrew Bible." In *Teaching the Bible: The Discourses and Politics of Biblical Pedagogy,* edited by Fernando F. Segovia and Mary Ann Tolbert, 105–16. Maryknoll, NY: Orbis, 1998.

———. "The Lesson of the Gibeonites: A Proposal for Dialogic Attention as a Strategy for Reading the Bible." In *Hispanic/Latino Theology: Challenge and Promise,* edited by Ada María Isasi-Díaz and Fernando F. Segovia, 73–85. Minneapolis: Fortress, 1995.

———. "Reading the Hyphens: An Emerging Biblical Hermeneutics for Latino/Hispanic U.S. Protestants." In *Protestantes/Protestants: Hispanic Christianity Within Mainline Traditions,* edited by David Maldonado, Jr., 160–173. Nashville: Abingdon, 1999.

———. "El Señor guarda a los emigrantes (Salmo 146:3)." In *Voces: Voices from the Hispanic Church,* edited by Justo L. González, 35–39. Nashville: Abingdon, 1992.

Goizueta, Roberto S., editor. *We Are a People: Initiatives in Hispanic American Theology.* Minneapolis: Fortress, 1992.

González, Justo L. *Mañana: Christian Theology from a Hispanic Perspective.* Nashville: Abingdon, 1990.

———. "Metamodern Aliens in Postmodern Jerusalem." In *Hispanic/Latino Theology: Challenge and Promise,* edited by Ada María Isasi-Díaz and Fernando F. Segovia, 340–50. Minneapolis: Fortress, 1995.

Hispanic Biblical Hermeneutics and Homiletics: A Brief Bibliography

———. "Pluralismo, justicia y misión: un estudio bíblico sobre Hechos 6:1–7." *Apuntes* 10 (1990) 3–8.

———. "Reading from My Bicultural Place: Acts 6:1–7." In *Reading from This Place*, edited by Fernando F. Segovia and Mary Ann Colbert, 1:139–48. Minneapolis: Fortress, 1995.

———. "Reinventing Dogmatics: A Footnote from a Reinvented Protestant." In *From the Heart of Our People: Latino/a Explorations in Catholic Systematic Theology*, edited by Orlando O. Espín and Miguel H. Díaz, 121–52. Maryknoll, NY: Orbis, 1999.

———. *Santa Biblia: Reading the Bible through Hispanic Eyes*. Nashville: Abingdon, 1995.

———. "Scripture, Tradition, Experience, and Imagination: A Redefinition." In *The Ties that Binds: African American and Hispanic American/Latino/a Theologies in Dialogue*, edited by Anthony B. Pinn and Benjamín Valentín, 61–73. New York: Continuum, 2001.

González, Justo L., and Catherine G. González. *The Liberating Pulpit*. Nashville: Abingdon, 1994.

González, Justo L., and Pablo A. Jiménez. *Púlpito: An Introduction to Hispanic Preaching*. Nashville: Abingdon, 2005.

Guardiola-Sáenz, Leticia A. "Scriptures." In *Handbook of Latino/a Theologies*, edited by Edwin David Aponte and Miguel A. De La Torre, 75–81. St. Louis: Chalice, 2006.

Gutierrez, Angel Luis, editor. *Voces del Púlpito Hispano*. Valley Forge, PA: Judson, 1989.

Isasi-Díaz, Ada María, and Fernando F. Segovia, editors. *Hispanic/Latino Theology: Challenge and Promise*. Minneapolis: Fortress, 1996.

Isasi-Díaz, Ada María. "Apuntes for a Hispanic Women's Theology of Liberation." *Apuntes* 6 (1986) 61–71.

———. "The Bible and Mujerista Theology." In *Lift Every Voice: Constructing Theologies from the Underside*, edited by Susan Brooks Thistlethwaite and Mary Potter Engel, 261–69. San Francisco: Harper & Row, 1990.

———. "'By the Rivers of Babylon': Exile as a Way of Life." In *Reading from This Place*, edited by Fernando F. Segovia and Mary Ann Tolbert, 1:149–63. Minneapolis: Fortress, 1995.

———. "Lo Cotidiano: A Key Element of Mujerista Theology." *Journal of Hispanic/Latino Theology* 10/1 (2002) 5–17.

———. *En la Lucha: In the Struggle: A Hispanic Women's Liberation Theology*. Minneapolis: Fortress, 1993.

———. *La Lucha Continues: Mujerista Theology*. Maryknoll, NY: Orbis, 2004.

———. "La Palabra de Dios en nosotras: The Word of God in Us." In *Searching the Scriptures*, edited by E. Schüssler Fiorenza, 1:86–100. New York: Crossroad, 1993.

Jiménez, Pablo A., and Justo L. González. *Manual de Homilética Hispana: Teoría y Práctica desde la Diáspora*. Barcelona: Clie, 2006.

Appendix

Jiménez, Pablo A. "The Bible: A Hispanic Perspective." In *Teología en Conjunto: A Collaborative Hispanic Protestant Theology*, edited by José David Rodríguez and Loida I. Martell-Otero, 66–79. Louisville: Westminster John Knox, 1997.

———. "In Search of a Hispanic Model of Biblical Interpretation." *Journal of Hispanic/Latino Theology* 3 (1995) 44–64.

———, editor. *Lumbrera a nuestro camino*. Miami: Caribe, 1994.

———. *La predicación en el siglo XXI: Homilética Liberacional y Contextual*. Barcelona: Clie, 2009.

———. *Principios de predicación*. Nashville: Abingdon, 2003.

López, Ediberto. "The Hermeneutical Process: Between Two Shores." *Apuntes* 24/3 (2004) 84–100.

Maldonado, Jorge, and Juan F. Martínez, editors. *Vivir y Servir en el Exilio: Lecturas Teológicas de la Experiencia Latina en los Estados Unidos*. Buenos Aires: Kairós, 2008.

Martell-Otero, Loida I. "Women Doing Theology: Una Perspectiva Evangélica." *Apuntes* 14 (1994) 67–85.

Martínez, Aquiles Ernesto. "Interpretación Bíblica y Postmodernidad con Sabor Latino." *Apuntes* 23/1 (2003) 4–27.

———. "Old Testament Legislation and Foreigners: An Alternative Majority Group Response." *Journal of Hispanic/Latino Theology* (2011). Online: http://www.latinotheology.org/2007/treatmentNofNforeigners.

Matovina, Timothy, editor. *Beyond Borders: Writings of Virgilio Elizondo and Friends*. Maryknoll, NY: Orbis, 2000.

Motessi, Osvaldo. *Predicación y Misión: Una Perspectiva Pastoral*. Miami: Logoi, 1989.

Pagán, Samuel. *Apocalipsis: Visión y Misión*. Miami: Caribe, 1993.

———. *Púlpito, Teología y Esperanza*. Miami: Caribe, 1988.

———. *Su Presencia en la Ausencia*. Miami: Caribe, 1993.

———. *El Tiempo Está Cerca: Una Lectura Pastoral del Apocalipsis*. Nashville: Caribe, 1999.

———, editor. *En Torno a Don Quijote y la teología: Inauguración del presidente del Seminario Evangélico de Puerto Rico*. San Juan, Puerto Rico: Seminario Evangélico de Puerto Rico, 1996.

———. *La Visión de Isaías*. Nashville: Caribe, 1997.

———. *Yo sé Quien Soy: Don Quijote para Creyentes, Soñadores y Visionarios*. San Juan, Puerto Rico: Seminario Evangélico de Puerto Rico, 1997.

Pedraja, Luis G. *Jesus Is My Uncle: Christology from a Hispanic Perspective*. Nashville: Abingdon, 1999.

Recinos, Harold J. *Hear the Cry! A Latino Pastor Challenges the Church*. Louisville: Westminster John Knox, 1989.

———. *Jesus Weeps: Global Encounters in Our Doorstep*. Nashville: Abingdon, 1992.

———. *Who Comes in the Name of the Lord?* Nashville: Abingdon, 1997.

Hispanic Biblical Hermeneutics and Homiletics: A Brief Bibliography

Richard, Pablo. "The Hermeneutics of Liberation: Theoretical Grounding for the Communitarian Reading of the Bible." In *Teaching the Bible: The Discourses and Politics of Biblical Pedagogy*, edited by Fernando F. Segovia and Mary Ann Tolbert, 272–82. Maryknoll, NY: Orbis, 1998.

Rivera-Rodríguez, Luis R. "Reading in Spanish from the Diaspora Through Hispanic Eyes." *Theology Today* 54 (1998) 480–90.

Rodríguez, José David, and Loida I. Martell-Otero, editors. *Teología en Conjunto: A Collaborative Hispanic Protestant Theology*. Louisville: Westminster John Knox, 1997.

Rodríguez, José David. "Confessing the Faith from a Hispanic Perspective." In *Protestantes/Protestants: Hispanic Christianity within Mainline Traditions*, edited by David Maldonado, Jr., 107–22. Nashville: Abingdon, 1999.

———. "Confessing the Faith in Spanish: Challenge and Prom-ise." In *Hispanic Theology: Challenge or Promise*, edited by Ada María Isasi-Díaz and Fernando F. Segovia, 351–66. Minneapolis: Fortress, 1995.

———. "The Parable of the Affirmative Action Employer." *Apuntes* 8 (1988) 51–59.

Rodríguez-Díaz, Daniel, editor. *Predicación Evangélica y Justicia Social*. Mexico: El Faro, 1994.

Romero, C. G. "Amos 5:21–24: Religion, Politics, and Latino Experience." *Journal of Hispanic/Latino Theology* 4 (1997) 21–41.

Rossing, John P. "*Mestizaje* and Marginality: A Hispanic American Theology" *Theology Today* 45/3 (1988) 293–304

Ruiz, Jean-Pierre. "Among the Exiles by the River Chebar: A U.S. Hispanic American Reading of Prophetic Cosmology in Ezekiel 1:1–3." *Journal of Hispanic/ Latino Theology* 6/2 (1998) 43–67.

———. "Beginning to Read the Bible in Spanish: An Initial Assessment." *Journal of Hispanic/ Latino Theology* 1 (1994) 28–50.

———. "The Bible and U.S. Hispanic American Theological Discourse." In *From the Heart of Our People: Latino/a Explorations in Catholic Systematic Theology*, edited by Orlando O. Espín and Miguel H. Díaz, 121–52. Maryknoll, NY: Orbis, 1999.

———. "The Bible and U.S. Hispanic American Theological Dis-course . . . Lessons from a Non-Innocent History." In *From the Heart of Our People: Latino/a Explorations in Catholic Systematic Theology*, edited by Orlando O. Espín and Miguel H. Díaz, 100–120. Maryknoll, NY: Orbis, 1999.

———. "Biblical Interpretation from a U.S. Hispanic American Perspective: A Reading of the Apocalypse." In *Cuerpo de Cristo: The Hispanic Presence in the U.S. Catholic Church*, edited by Peter Casarella and Raúl Gómez, 78–105. New York: Crossroad, 1998.

Segovia, Fernando F. "And They Began to Speak in Other Tongues: Competing Modes of Discourse in Contemporary Biblical Criticism." In *Reading from This Place*, edited by Fernando F. Segovia and Mary Ann Tolbert, 1:1–32. Minneapolis: Fortress, 1995.

Appendix

———. "Cultural Studies and Contemporary Biblical Criticism: Ideological Criticism as Mode of Discourse." In *Reading from This Place*, edited by Fernando F. Segovia and Mary Ann Tolbert, 2:1–17. Minneapolis: Fortress, 1995.

———. *Decolonizing Biblical Studies: A View from the Margins*. Maryknoll, NY: Orbis, 2000.

———. "Hispanic American Theology and the Bible: Effective Weapon and Faithful Ally." In *We Are a People!: Initiatives in Hispanic American Theology*, edited by Roberto S. Goizueta, 21–29. Minneapolis: Fortress, 1992.

———. "A New Manifest Destiny: The Emerging Theological Voice of Hispanic Americans." *Religious Studies Review* 17 (1991) 101–9.

———. "Pedagogical Discourse and Practices in Cultural Studies: Toward a Contextual Biblical Pedagogy." In *Teaching the Bible: The Discourses and Politics of Biblical Pedagogy*, edited by Fernando F. Segovia and Mary Ann Tolbert, 137–167. Maryknoll, NY: Orbis, 1998.

———. "Reading the Bible as Hispanic Americans." In *The New Interpreter's Bible*, 1:167–173. Nashville: Abingdon, 1994.

———. "The Text as Other: Toward a Hispanic American Herme-neutics." In *Text and Experience: Toward a Cultural Exegesis of the Bible*. Edited by Daniel Christopher-Smith, 276–98. Biblical Seminar 35. Sheffield: JSOT Press, 1995.

———. "Toward a Hermeneutics of the Diaspora: A Hermeneutics of Otherness and Engagement." In *Reading from This Place*, edited by Fernando F. Segovia and Mary Ann Tolbert, 1:57–73. Minneapolis: Fortress, 1995.

———. "Toward Intercultural Criticism: A Reading Strategy from the Diaspora." In *Reading from This Place*, edited by Fernando F. Segovia and Mary Ann Tolbert, 2:303–330. Minneapolis: Fortress, 1995.

Trainor, Michael. "Intertextuality, the Hermeneutics of 'Other,' and Mark 16:6–7: A New but not New Challenge for Biblical Interpreters." *Biblical Theology Bulletin* 35 (2005) 144–50. Online: btb.sagepub.com/content/35/4.toc.

Bibliography

Adam, A. K. M., editor *Handbook of Postmodern Biblical Interpretation*. St. Louis: Chalice, 2000.
Adam, Margaret B. "This is *My* Story, This is *My* Song . . . A Feminist Claim on Scripture, Ideology and Interpretation." In *Escaping Eden: New Feminist Perspectives on the Bible*, edited by Harold C. Washington, et al., 218–32. Biblical Seminar 65. Sheffield: Sheffield Academic, 1998.
Alcoff, Linda. "The Problem of Speaking for Others." *Cultural Critique* 20 (1991) 5–32.
Allen, Bob. "Baptists Split on NC Gay Marriage Ban." ABP News, May 9, 2012. Online: http://www.abpnews.com/culture/social-issues/item/7370-baptists-split-on-nc-gay-marriage-ban#.UZJYs6LVUxE.
Allen, Ronald J. "Assessing the Authority of a Sermon." *Encounter* 67 (2006) 63–74.
———. *Hearing the Sermon: Relationship, Content, Feeling*. St. Louis: Chalice, 2004.
———."How Do People Listen to Sermons?" *Preaching* 21 (2005) 52–55.
———. "Is Preaching Caught or Taught? How Practitioners Learn." *Theological Education* 41 (2005) 137–52.
———. "Preaching after a Tragedy: Listening to Congregations after September 11, 2001." *Encounter* 66 (2005) 221–32.
———. "Preaching to Listeners: What Listeners Most Value in Sermons." *Homiletics* 17 (2005) 7.
———. "Three Settings on which People Hear Sermons." *Lectionary Homiletics* 16 (2004–5) 1–3.
———. "What Do Lay People Think God is Doing in the Sermon?" *Encounter* 66 (2005) 365–75.
———. "What Makes Preaching Disciples Preaching?" *DisciplesWorld* 4 (2005) 28–39.
Allen, Ronald J., and Mary Alice Mulligan. *Make the Word Come Alive: Lessons from Laity*. St. Louis: Chalice, 2006.

Bibliography

Asad, Talal. "Remarks on the Anthropology of the Body." In *Religion and the Body*, edited by Sarah Coakley, 42–52. Cambridge Studies in Religious Traditions 8. Cambridge: Cambridge University Press, 1997.

Atkinson, Lucy Rose. *Sharing the Word: Preaching and the Round-Table Church*. Louisville: Westminster John Knox, 1997.

Baab, Lynne M. *Personality Type in Congregations: How to Work with Others More Effectively*. Herndon, VA: Alban, 1998.

Bailey, Clinton. *Bedouin Poetry from Sinai to the Negev: Mirror of a Culture*. Oxford: Clarendon, 1991.

Barr, James. "Some Thoughts on Narrative, Myth, and Incarnation." In *God Incarnate: Story and Belief*, edited by Anthony Ernest Harvey, 14–23. London: SPCK, 1991.

———. *The Scope and Authority of the Bible*. London: SCM, 1980.

Barth, Karl. *Church Dogmatics*, vol. 1/2, *The Doctrine of the Word of God*, edited by G. W. Bromiley and T. F. Torrance, and translated by G. T. Thomson and Harold Knight. Edinburgh: T. & T. Clark, 1957.

Bartlett, David L. *Between the Bible and the Church: New Methods for Biblical Preaching*. Nashville: Abingdon, 1999.

Benjamin, Walter. *Illuminations*. Translated by Harry Zohn. Edited by Hannah Arendt. 1968. Reprinted, London: Fontana, 1992.

Black, Kathy. *A Healing Homiletic: Preaching and Disability*. Nashville: Abingdon, 1996.

Bourdieu, Pierre. *Outline of A Theory of Practice*. London: Cambridge University Press, 1977.

Brauch, Manfred T. *Abusing Scripture: The Consequences of Misreading the Bible*. Downers Grove, IL: InterVarsity, 2009.

Bridgeman Davis, Valerie. "Response in Prose and Poetry." *Semeia* 72 (1995) 215–16.

Brink, Andre. *A Chain of Voices*. Naperville, IL: Sourcebooks, 2007.

Brown, Kelly D. "God Is As Christ Does: Toward a Womanist Theology." *Journal of Religious Thought* 46 (1989) 7–16.

Brown, Raymond E. *An Introduction to the Gospel of John*, edited by Francis J. Moloney. Anchor Bible Reference Library. New York: Doubleday, 2003.

———. *The Gospel according to John I–XII*. Anchor Bible 29. Garden City, NY: Doubleday, 1966.

Brueggemann, Walter. *Finally Comes the Poet: Daring Speech for Proclamation*. Minneapolis: Fortress, 1989.

———. *Texts Under Negotiation: The Bible and Postmodern Imagination*. Minneapolis: Fortress, 1993.

———. *Theology of the Old Testament: Testimony, Dispute, Advocacy*. Minneapolis: Fortress, 1997.

Burke, Kenneth. *A Rhetoric of Motives*. Berkeley: University of California Press, 1969.

Butler, Judith. *Excitable Speech*. London: Routledge, 1997.

———. "Performative Acts and Gender Constitution." In *The Twentieth-Century Performance Reader*, 2nd ed., edited by Michael Huxley and Noel Watts, 154–65. London: Routledge, 2002.

Calinescu, Matei. "Orality in Literacy: Some Historical Paradoxes of Reading." *Yale Journal of Criticism* 6 (1993) 175–90.

———. *Rereading*. New Haven: Yale University Press, 1993.

Carlson, Marvin. *Performance: A Critical Introduction*. 2nd ed. New York: Routledge, 2004.

Campbell, Charles L. *Preaching Jesus: New Directions for Homiletics in Hans Frei's Postliberal Theology*. Grand Rapids: Eerdmans, 1997.

Cannon, Katie. "The Emergence of Black Feminist Consciousness." In *Feminist Interpretations of the Bible*, edited by Letty Russell, 30–40. Philadelphia: Westminster, 1985.

Charles, Tyler. "Thumb Wars." *Leadership Journal* (2010). Online: http://www.christianitytoday.com/le/2010/winter/thumbwars.html.

Chopp, Rebecca. *The Power to Speak: Feminism, Language, God*. New York: Crossroad, 1989.

Clark-Soles, Jaime. *Engaging the Word: The New Testament and the Christian Believer*. Louisville: Westminster John Knox, 2010.

Claypool, John R. *The Preaching Event: The Lyman Beecher Lectures*. Waco, TX: Word, 1980.

———. *Tracks of a Fellow Struggler: How to Handle Grief*. Waco, TX: Word, 1974.

Clines, David J. A. *Interested Parties: The Ideology of Writers and Readers of the Hebrew Bible*. JSOTSup 205. Sheffield: Sheffield Academic, 1995.

Coakley, Sarah. *Powers and Submissions: Spirituality, Philosophy, and Gender*. Malden, MA: Blackwell, 2002.

Cole, Johnnetta B. "Jesus Is a Sister." In *My Soul Is a Witness: African-American Women's Spirituality*, edited by Gloria Wade-Gayles, 156–60. Boston: Beacon, 1995.

Cone, James H., and Gayraud S. Wilmore. *Black Theology: A Documentary History*, vol. 2, *1980–1992*. Maryknoll, NY: Orbis, 1993.

Craddock, Fred B. *As One without Authority*. Nashville: Abingdon, 1979.

Daniel, Lillian. *Telling It Like It Is: Reclaiming the Practice of Testimony*. Herndon, VA: Alban, 2006.

Davis, Ellen F. "Teaching the Bible Confessionally in the Church." In *The Art of Reading Scripture*, edited by Ellen F. Davis and Richard B. Hays, 9–26. Grand Rapids: Eerdmans, 2003.

———. *Wondrous Depth: Preaching the Old Testament*. Louisville: Westminster John Knox, 2005.

Dewey, Joanna. "The Gospel of John in Its Oral–Written Media World." In *Jesus in Johannine Tradition*, edited by Robert T. Fortna and Tom Thatcher, 239–52. Louisville: Westminster John Knox, 2002.

Dietrich, Walter, and Ulrich Luz. *The Bible in a World Context: An Experiment in Contextual Hermeneutics*. Grand Rapids: Eerdmans, 2002.

Bibliography

Durrah, Betty J. "Triple Jeopardy: The Impact of Race, Sex, and Class on Women of Color." *Church and Society* 82 (1991) 44–53.

Dykstra, Craig. *Growing in the Life of Faith*. Louisville: Westminster John Knox, 1999.

Eusebius. *The History of the Church*. Translated by G. A. Williamson. New York: Dorset, 1984.

Fish, Stanley E. *Is There a Text in This Class? Authority of Interpretative Communities*. Cambridge: Harvard University Press, 1980.

Flake, Elaine M. *God in Her Midst: Preaching Healing to Wounded Women*. Valley Forge, PA: Judson, 2007.

Florence, Anna Carter. *Preaching as Testimony*. Louisville: Westminster John Knox, 2007.

Foster, Hal. *Postmodern Culture*. London: Pluto, 1985.

Frei, Hans. *The Eclipse of Biblical Narrative*. New Haven: Yale University Press, 1980.

Fulkerson, Mary McClintock. *Changing the Subject: Women's Discourses and Feminist Theology*. Minneapolis: Fortress, 1994.

González, Justo L. *Mañana: Christian Theology from a Hispanic Perspective*. Nashville: Abingdon, 1990.

———. "Metamodern Aliens in Postmodern Jerusalem." In *Hispanic/Latino Theology: Challenge and Promise*, edited by Ada María Isasi-Díaz and Fernando F. Segovia, 340–50. Minneapolis: Fortress, 1995.

———. *Santa Biblia: Reading the Bible through Hispanic Eyes*. Nashville: Abingdon, 1995.

González, Justo L., and Pablo A. Jiménez. *Púlpito: An Introduction to Hispanic Preaching*. Nashville: Abingdon, 2005.

Gowan, Donald E. "Wealth and Poverty in the Old Testament: The Care of the Widow, the Orphan, and the Sojourner." *Interpretation* 41 (1984) 341–53.

Grant, Jacquelyn. *White Women's Christ and Black Women's Jesus: Feminist Christology and Womanist Response*. Atlanta: Scholars, 1989.

Hanson, Paul D. *A People Called: The Growth of Community in the Bible*. San Francisco: Harper & Row, 1986.

Hauerwas, Stanley. *Performing the Faith: Bonhoeffer and the Practice of Nonviolence*. Grand Rapids: Brazos, 2004.

Hewison, Robert. *The Heritage Industry: Britain in a Climate of Decline*. London: Methuen, 1988.

Holmes, Zan. "Enabling the Word to Happen." In *Power in the Pulpit: How America's Most Effective Black Preachers Prepare Their Sermons*, edited by Cleophus J. LaRue, 74–82. Louisville: Westminster John Knox, 2002.

Hylen, Susan E. *Imperfect Believers: Ambiguous Characters in the Gospel of John*. Louisville: Westminster John Knox, 2009.

Isasi-Díaz, Ada María. "The Bible and Mujerista Theology." In *Lift Every Voice: Constructing Theologies from the Underside*, edited by Susan Brooks Thistlethwaite and Mary Potter Engel, 267–75. San Francisco: Harper & Row, 1990.

Bibliography

———. *La Lucha Continues: Mujerista Theology*. Maryknoll, NY: Orbis, 2004.
———. "La Palabra de Dios en nosotras: The Word of God in Us." In *Searching the Scriptures*, edited by Elisabeth Schüssler Fiorenza, 1:86–100. New York: Crossroad, 1993.
Jenson, Robert A. *Telling the Story: Variety and Imagination in Preaching*. Philadelphia: Fortress, 1980.
Jiménez, Pablo A. *La Predicación en el siglo XXI: Homilética liberacional y contextual*. Barcelona: Clie, 2009.
Käsemann, Ernst. *The Testament of Jesus: According to John 17*. Translated by Gerhard Krodel. Philadelphia: Fortress, 1966.
Kellerman, Diether. "*gur*." In *TDOT*, 2:439–49.
Kershaw, Baz. *The Radical in Performance: Between Brecht and Baudrillard*. 1st ed. New York: Routledge, 1999.
Kim, Matthew D. *Preaching to Second Generation Korean Americans: Toward a Possible Selves Contextual Homiletic*. American University Studies. Series VII, Theology and Religion 265. New York: Lang, 2007.
Lemche, Niels Peter. *The Old Testament between Theology and History: A Critical Survey*. Louisville: Westminster John Knox, 2008.
Levinas, Emmanuel. *Totality and Infinity: An Essay on Exteriority*. Pittsburgh: Duquesne University Press, 1969.
Lewis, Karoline M. *Rereading the Shepherd Discourse: Restoring the Integrity of John 9:39—10:21*. Studies in Biblical Literature 113. New York: Lang, 2008.
Lincoln, Andrew T. *Truth on Trial: The Lawsuit Motif in the Fourth Gospel*. Peabody, MA: Hendrickson, 2000.
Lischer, Richard. *A Theology of Preaching: The Dynamics of the Gospel*. Durham, NC: Labyrinth, 1992.
Long, Thomas G. *Testimony: Talking Ourselves into Being Christian*. Practices of Faith Series. San Francisco: Jossey-Bass, 2004.
———. *The Witness of Preaching*. 2nd ed. Louisville: Westminster John Knox, 2005.
Lorde, Audre. "Sexism: An American Disease in Blackface." In *Sister Outsider: Essays and Speeches by Audre Lorde*, 60–65. Freedom, CA: Crossing, 1984.
Lowry, Eugene L. *The Homiletical Plot: The Sermon as Narrative Art Form*. Expanded ed. Louisville: Westminster John Knox, 2001.
Lughood, Lila Abu. *Veiled Sentiments: Honor and Poetry in the Bedouin Society*. Berkeley: University of California Press, 1986.
Malina, Bruce J. "Hospitality." In *Handbook of Biblical Social Values*, edited by John J. Pilch and Bruce Malina, 115–18. Peabody, MA: Hendrickson, 1998.
Martin-Achard, R. "*gvr*." In *TLOT* 1:307–10.
McClure, John S. *The Round-Table Pulpit: Where Leadership and Preaching Meet*. Nashville: Abingdon, 1995.
———. "The Practice of Sermon Listening." *Congregations* (2006) 6–9.
McClure, John S., et al. *Listening to Listeners: Homiletical Case Studies*. St. Louis: Chalice, 2004.

Bibliography

McClure, John, and Nancy Ramsay. *Telling the Truth: Preaching about Sexual and Domestic Violence.* Cleveland: United Church, 1998.

Meek, Theophile James. "The Translation of GER in the Hexateuch and Its Bearing on the Documentary Hypothesis." *Journal of Biblical Literature* 49 (1930) 172–80.

Meeks, Wayne. "The Man from Heaven in Johannine Sectarianism." *Journal of Biblical Literature* 91 (1972) 44–72.

Monteith, Margo, and Jeffrey Winters. "Why We Hate." *Psychology Today* 35 (2002) 44–51, 87.

Meyers, Robin R. *With Ears to Hear: Preaching as Self-persuasion.* Cleveland: Pilgrim, 1993.

Nieman, James R., and Thomas G. Rogers. *Preaching to Every Pew: Cross-cultural Strategies.* Minneapolis: Fortress, 2001.

Nunn, Brittany. "Teens Sacrifice 'Want' To Meet Needs." Amarillo Globe-News, December 23, 2011. Online: http://amarillo.com/news/local-news/2011-12-23/teens-sacrifice-want-meet-needs.

O'Day, Gail. *The Gospel of John.* In *New Interpreter's Bible* 9. Nashville: Abingdon, 1995.

Oden, Amy G., editor. *And You Welcomed Me: A Sourcebook on Hospitality in Early Christianity.* Nashville: Abingdon, 2001.

Ottoni-Wilhelm, Dawn. "New Hermeneutic, New Homiletic, and New Directions: An U.S.–North American Perspective." *Homiletic* 35 (2010) 17–31.

Patte, Daniel. *Ethics of Biblical Interpretation: A Re-evaluation.* Louisville: Westminster John Knox, 1993.

Patte, Daniel, et al. *The Gospel of Matthew: A Contextual Introduction for Group Study.* Nashville: Abingdon, 2002.

Patterson, Richard D. "The Widow, the Orphan, and the Poor in the Old Testament and Extra-biblical Literature." *Bibliotheca Sacra* 130/519 (1973) 223–34

Penchansky, David. "Up for Grabs: A Tentative Proposal for Doing Ideological Criticism." *Semeia* 59 (1992) 35–41.

Pohl, Christine D. *Making Room: Recovering Hospitality as a Christian Tradition.* Grand Rapids: Eerdmans, 1999.

Quintilian. *The Orator's Education (Institutio Oratoria).* Vol. 4, Books 9–10. Edited and translated by Donald A. Russell. Loeb Classical Library. Cambridge: Harvard University Press, 2001.

Rahner, Karl. "Priest and Poet." In *Theological Investigations*, 3:253–86. Translated by Karl H. Kruger and Boniface Kruger. Baltimore: Helicon, 1967.

———. "The Word of God and the Eucharist." In *Theological Investigations*, 4:287–311. Translated by David Bourke. Baltimore: Helicon, 1966.

Reinhartz, Adele. *Befriending the Beloved Disciple: A Jewish Reading of the Gospel of John.* New York: Continuum, 2003.

Ricoeur, Paul. "The Hermeneutics of Testimony." In *Essays on Biblical Interpretation*, translated by David Stewart and Charles E. Reagan, 78–101. Philadelphia: Fortress, 1980.

Bibliography

Rodríguez, José David, and Loida I. Martell-Otero, editors. *Teología en conjunto: A Collaborative Hispanic Protestant Theology*. Louisville: Westminster John Knox, 1997.
Sanders, James A. *Canon and Community: A Guide to Canonical Criticism*. Guides to Biblical Scholarship. Philadelphia: Fortress, 1984.
———. *From Sacred Story to Sacred Text*. Philadelphia: Fortress, 1987.
Segovia, Fernando F. *Decolonizing Biblical Studies: A View from the Margins*. Maryknoll, NY: Orbis, 2004.
———. *Reading from This Place: Social Location and Biblical Interpretation in the United States*. Minneapolis: Fortress, 1995.
Seitz, Christopher R. *Zion's Final Destiny: The Development of the Book of Isaiah: A Reassessment of Isaiah 36–39*. Minneapolis: Fortress, 1991.
Smith, Christine. *Preaching as Weeping, Confession, and Resistance: Radical Responses to Radical Evil*. Louisville: Westminster John Knox, 1992.
Soulen, Richard N., and R. Kendall Soulen. *Handbook of Biblical Criticism*. 3rd ed. Louisville: Westminster John Knox, 2001.
Steimle, Edmund, et al. *Preaching the Story*. 1980. Reprinted, Eugene, OR: Wipf & Stock, 2003.
Stewart, John Robert. *Language as Articulate Contact: Toward a Post-Semiotic Philosophy of Communication*. SUNY Series in Speech Communication. Albany: SUNY Press, 1995.
Taylor, Barbara Brown, *The Preaching Life*. Cambridge: Cowley, 1993.
Thompson, William M. *The Struggle for Theology's Soul: Contesting Scripture in Christology*. New York: Crossroad, 1996.
Tisdale, Leonora Tubbs. *Preaching as Local Theology and Folk Art*. Fortress Resources for Preaching. Minneapolis: Fortress, 1997.
Townes, Emilie M. "A Black Feminist Critique of Feminist Theology." *Wesleyan Theology Today* (1985) 189–91.
———. "Introduction: On Creating Ruminations from the Soul." In *A Troubling in My Soul: Womanist Perspectives on Evil & Suffering*, edited by Emilie M. Townes, 1–11. Maryknoll, NY: Orbis, 1993.
———. "Searching for Paradise in a World of Theme Parks." In *Black Faith and Public Talk: Critical Essays on James H. Cone's Black Theology and Black Power*, edited by Dwight N. Hopkins, 105–25. Maryknoll, NY: Orbis, 1999.
Troeger, Thomas H., and H. Edward Everding Jr. *So That All Might Know: Preaching that Engages the Whole Congregation*. Nashville: Abingdon, 2008.
Turner-Sharraz, Diane, et al. *Believing in Preaching: What Listeners Hear in Preaching*. St. Louis: Chalice, 2005.
———. "The 'So What' Factor in the Sermon: How the Sermon Connects." *Journal of Theology* (2005) 45–58.
Vaux, Roland de. *Ancient Israel*. Vol. 1, *Social Institutions*. Translated by John McHugh. New York: McGraw-Hill, 1965.
Walker, Alice. *The Color Purple*. Boston: Mariner, 2006.
Webster's New Collegiate Dictionary. Springfield, MA: Merriam, 1977.

Bibliography

Weems, Renita J. "Do You See What I See? Diversity in Interpretation." *Journal of Church and Society* 82 (1991) 28–43.

———. "How Will Our Preaching Be Remembered? A Challenge to See the Bible from a Woman's Perspective." *The African American Pulpit* (2006) 26–29.

———. "Reading *Her* Way through the Struggle." In *Stony the Road We Trod: African American Biblical Interpretation*, edited by Cain Hope Felder, 57–80. Minneapolis: Fortress, 1991.

Wiesel, Elie. "The Holocaust as Literary Inspiration." In Elie Wiesel, et al., *Dimensions of the Holocaust: Lectures at Northwestern University*, 5–19. Evanston: Northwestern University Press, 1977.

———. *The Jews of Silence: A Personal Report on Soviet Jewry*. New York: Schocken, 1987.

Williams, Delores. "The Color of Feminism: Or 'Speaking The Black Woman's Tongue.'" *Journal of Religious Thought* 43 (1986) 2–58.

Williams, Rowan. *Tokens of Trust: An Introduction to Christian Belief*. Louisville: Westminster John Knox, 2007.

Willimon, William H. *The Intrusive Word: Preaching to the Unbaptized*. Grand Rapids: Eerdmans, 1992.

Willimon, William H., and Stanley Hauerwas. *Preaching to Strangers*. Louisville: Westminster John Knox, 1992.

Wilson, Paul Scott. *The Practice of Preaching*. Rev. ed. Nashville: Abingdon, 2007.

www.ingramcontent.com/pod-product-compliance
Lightning Source LLC
Chambersburg PA
CBHW050819160426
43192CB00010B/1825